Written by Dom Kennell

Dedicated to:
Amelia Hall, Jess Olds and, last but by no means least, James Adam.
I hope you enjoy this slice of absurdity.

Chapter One-liest

An Uninvited Guest

What makes the world go round? Is it love? Perhaps, it's money. Well…some think that *stories* make the world go round. And this one? This is a particularly good one and it all started not so long ago…

***

A rusty antique bell rang loudly and echoed into the dusty shop. The air was thick and smelt of old books. Long red velvet curtains with grubby gold tassels were drawn so tightly together than only tiny slithers of sunlight could fight their way into the shop. A faint ticking of a clock broke the silence.

"Hello? Hello? Anyone there?" Noah wandered further into the room.

Each step Noah took rumbled on the floor in such a way that the ornaments which were crammed onto each shelf seemed to wobble slightly as though they may crash down at any point. Tiny white dinosaurs plant pots and large ceramic mice were overshadowed by jars of various colours and shapes.

"Hot chocolate?" A wheezy voice rasped behind him.

Noah spun round. A stout man with a wispy moustache and multicoloured dungarees stood behind the worn oak counter. The fez he wore precariously on his head completely clashed with the patterns on his dungarees but somehow his carefree manner pulled it off quite magnificently.

"Where did you come from?" Noah demanded.

"Hot chocolate?" The shop keeper asked again, apparently ignoring the indignation in Noah's voice. The elderly man pulled out an enormous tea pot (with a pattern of chickens painted onto it) from behind the counter and set it down with a small clank. Next, he pulled out a pair of miniature chipped teacups and saucers and placed them down with an echoing clink. He arched his eyebrows as though waiting patiently for a response. (Noah, however, was too busy goggling at the size of the teapot compared to the dainty teacups to notice he was meant to reply). The ticking of the clock seemed to thunder in the stuffy silence.

"Er…no thanks." Noah replied, finally processing that he had in fact been asked a question but answered it little less politely than he would have liked to a total stranger.

"Very well." The shop keeper shrugged and began to pour himself a large cupful of the hot beverage into a teacup. With an enormous flourish, the shop keeper pulled the teapot up *just* at the point when the chips in the china might have seeped through rivers of hotchocolate.

As Noah turned away to further inspect the shop, the sweet aroma of the comforting drink wafted through the air making Noah regret his decision immensely. Absently, as a way to distract himself from the rich inviting scent, he reached for the bookin front of him.

"Can I interest you in some Fishnell?" The shop keeper asked, tapping his teacup alittle too hard so a chunk of china snapped into his teacup, making a small *plop* sound.

"Fishnell?" Noah asked, turning his head back to the shop keeper. The shop keepers'footsteps were heavy and dragged slightly as he squinted to look closely at the battered books.

"Fishnell…Fishnell…Fish…Aha!" The plump man pulled a large heavy book with crumpled purple leather and peeling golden cursive writing. The shop keeper dusted the ancient book off and handed it to Noah. Noah grunted slightly under the weight of the book. (He then made a quick mental note to raise his weights at the gym as he concluded he shouldn't feel a book should be a workout.)

"Great adventure!" The shop keeper chirped gleefully as he dragged himself backtowards the counter. Noah flicked through the first few pages. Then the next few. Then afew more after that. The yellowing pages which curled slightly at the edges and groaned in pain with each careful page turn were completely blank. Almost as though the shop keeper could read Noah's thoughts, his eyes shone with a playful glint.

"A book doesn't need *words* for an adventure." The shop keeper smiled with an unnaturally large grin.

"So…it's a notebook?"

Before the shopkeeper could reply, a cuckoo clock chimed loudly, making

Noah jump out of his skin. He checked his watch then scrunched his faces into an annoyed grimace.

"Shoot, I'm late. How much for the…" Noah lifted the book into the air.

"What's your best offer?" The shop keeper replied tilting his head slightly and making the fez look like it had overcome the basic force of gravity.

"Err…" Noah reached into his jeans pocket. Empty. Grunting slightly, he switched the arm which was holding the book and checked his other pocket. The grand total of his pocket was his phone, a few coins, a piece of string, some fluff and a tissue so ripped it was almost a pile of fluff in itself. Quickly, Noah tallied up the coins.

"Fiver?" Noah offered as he extended his hand out slightly.

"Done." The shop keeper cheeped with his uncomfortably broad smile, taking the change, and knocking it into the cash register.

***

Lottie tutted at the enormous clock on the wall as she shook her head. With a heavy sigh she plated the small mountain of mash potato and sausages with an angry clatter and slopped onion gravy on the top of the meal in such a manner that was so tired that even the pigs in which the sausages were made for the dinner felt sorry for her. *Late again.* As Lottie dumped the plate onto the table and pulled out her chair with unnecessary force, the door opened.
"Hi, sorry, sorry!" Noah's apologies called from the hall.

"I was wondering where you were." Lottie shouted with an icy tone.

Within a few seconds Noah's mop of dark ringlets appeared at the door wearing a sheepish expression. The towering cold shoulder seemed to be amplified by the scraping of metal on porcelain as Lottie tucked into her meal.

"I'm sorry…" Noah murmured.

"Save it." Lottie retorted through a face full of creamy mashed potato.

"I needed to—" But Noah was saved from fabricating another excuse for his poor time keeping by the shrill call of the doorbell. As though she'd never head a doorbell before, Lottie's head snapped with an expression of total confusion.

"Who's that?" She demanded as she checked the time again. It was too late to be a casual neighbour dropping in for nothing serious.
"I dunno." Noah shrugged as he tried to seamlessly slip into the place at the table. Unfortunately, he got so tightly wedged between the table and his seat, Lottie was forced to pull the table towards herself slightly.

"I'll get it." Lottie huffed as she rolled her eyes.

Noah reached for the cold fork and began to shovel the food into his mouth with such force that when Lottie returned, she had to actively stop herself from rolling her eyes at him again.

"Who was it?" Noah enquired as he spat a small chunk of sausage across the table.

"No one." Lottie glowered back as she returned to her seat.

Knowing that Lottie's mood clearly was not going to shift any time soon, Noah seized the opportunity to try and make things better.

"Here." He chimed as brightly as he could, pulling out a poorly wrapped large brown paper package. Lottie narrowed her eye for a second but took the peace offering.

"What's this?"

"Surprise." Noah smiled, relieved that he might be off the hook. "I can be romantic you know." He added as he stuffed a whole large sausage into his mouth and chewed aggressively to manage the mouthful.

As gently as she could, Lottie peeled the tape away from the paper and pulled out a large heavy oblong shape.

"Adventures of Wheyshaven?" She asked, trying hard not to let the disappointment seep through in her tone.

"I know how much you love a notebook." Noah gloated, clearly more pleased with the gift than he should have been.

Ignoring the tone of Noah's comment, Lottie paged through the pages with such respect a person would have thought she was consulting a sacred script.

"It's lovely thank…what's this?"

"What?" Noah asked as he reached for the glass of juice in front of him. Lottie's bright eyes squinted tightly as she tried to make out the faded inky scrawls.

"Upon being summoned you are enlisted." Lottie read her voice was so hushed and so reverend it would not have been out of place as a silent cathedral. Noah's nose crinkled as his eyebrows knitted together in confusion. Lottie leant over for Noah to read.

"Upon being summoned you are enlisted." Noah mummed with thought of a person trying to figure out the answer to a hard crossword puzzle. His thought was boorishly interrupted by another shrill call from the doorbell.

Lottie's closed her eyes in way that signalled to Noah that if he didn't take this job, he would be back with the frosty tension that greeted him.

"I'll get it!" He said as sweetly as he could.

The chair scraped loudly on the tiled floor as Noah rose, wiping gravy from his patchy beard. Hastily, Noah half-jogged down the corridor and grabbed the door handle. Before Noah had time to make sense of the stranger on the doorstep, they lunged towards him grabbing his shoulders and began shaking him so violently he felt his brain rattle slightly.

"There's no time. Wheyshaven is in danger. Hurry!" The uninvited visitor squawked with a nasally voice.

Chapter Twolean

The Green Flamingo

Before Noah knew what had happened the tall green flamingo had muscled theirway through the front door muttering incoherently as its head spun in every direction as though looking for something.

"What—"

"There's no time. Hurry."

Noah didn't move but remained rooted to the spot, his jaw hanging so far from its joint that it was closer to the floor than the top of his head. Rolling their eyes with a clear sense of annoyance, the flamingo unzipped the satchel hanging over its shoulder and pulled out a small cube. The flamingo shook the cube roughly with a wing and with a loud click there was a *zap*.

"Ouch!" Noah yelped, rubbing his left ear.

"What's going on?" Lottie's voice wafted through from the kitchen.

"Wheyshaven is in danger, there's no time. Hurry!" The flamingo shrieked nasally as they pulled away the feathers from its wings like a sleeve to check the time on a series of different watches on its wrist. Rubbing his eyes, Noah caught a glance of the watches. Each one seemed to be going at different speeds and (or even more puzzlingly) different directions.

Lottie appeared in the doorframe. Her eyes widened as she gaped at the stranger in the house. Suddenly, the flamingo made a charge for the stairs and flew up them with alarming speed. Noah and Lottie just stared at each other.

"*Come on.*" The flamingo insisted, popping up from around the corner. Neither Lottie nor Noah moved. Two small clicks could be heard followed by two loud *zaps*.

"Ow!" Noah and Lottie shrieked as they rubbed their ears while the flamingos head disappeared again.

"Will you *stop* that?" Noah demanded as he shot the place where the flamingo's head had been a filthy glare.

"Come with me. There's no time to lose!" The pitched voice called.
"Should we go?" Lottie asked, her voice squeaky.

"Well, I don't want to be zapped again." Noah grumbled as he stomped towards the stairs.

With each step, Lottie and Noah could hear a running shower getting louder. By the top of the stairs, they could see steam streaming out the open door of the bathroom. The flamingo was scurrying about, its wings flailing about in such a way that the gangly creature somehow looked to be made of rubber.

"Now, which of you is the summonee?" The creature asked briskly as it rummaged through its satchel.

Lottie glanced at Noah who gave her a knowing side eye expression in return. From the satchel, the flamingo pulled a huge scroll of parchment that was far too big for the size of the satchel. The flamingo looked between Lottie and Noah, waiting. No one moved.

"Book please." The flamingo finally said in a sulky voice.

Lottie and Noah exchanged glance again and shrugged. The flamingos wing dropped to its side as its eyebrows arched.

"The book of Wheyshaven, where is it?"

"Er...downstairs?" Lottie said with a slight quiver in her voice.

"Downstairs? Downstairs? Goodtoads this is going to take forever." The flamingo burst with a flash of red in its eyes.

"Er...I'll get it." Noah offered as he half jumped down the stairs. It wasn't on the table. It wasn't on the counter.

"Where *is* it?" Noah began randomly opening draws and cupboards. After opening the cutlery drawer twice and the biscuit cupboard three times (though he would be lying if he said the third time was to actually look for the book as he plucked a custard cream from its packet), he turned around with a sigh. The book lay open on the tabletop next to his plate. *Odd.* Noah thought as he closed with a snap and grabbed it up, holding it close as he staggered up the stairs.

"Took you long enough." The flamingo muttered as it pulled the shower curtain open. "You," he pointed a long emerald feather towards Lottie, "come with me. You stay here and protect the book at all costs. If a cramfardle turns up remember, turn three times clockwise, half a turn anticlockwise and jump out with your arms out. It'll instantly explode."

"A *what?*" Noah shouted before he could stop himself. "You in here, now." The flamingo barked at Lottie sternly.

Reluctantly, she squeezed herself into the tiny cubicle with the bird. She hunched her shoulders together as the big bird wriggled for more room. "Now what?" Noah asked as his eyes flitted between Lottie and the flamingo.

"The book. No, no, no. Don't give it to me. *Read* from it." The flamingo answered, putting a wing to its beak as it closed its eyes and shook its head slightly.

"It's a blank book. There's nothing to read." Noah replied angrily.

"Just read the first chapter."

"But—"

"Just do it!" The flamingo scowled.

Shaking his head, Noah opened this book. His eyes widened in surprise and his head shot up from the first page.

"How is this—"

"Just read!" The flamingo instructed briskly.

"Upon the arrival of the collector--" Noah mumbled as his eyes strained to make out the what the handwriting was trying to convey.

"Louder." The flamingo interrupted.

Noah cleared his throat and took a deep breath. "Upon the arrival of the collector--"

"Wait!" The flamingo screeched as it hurriedly delved a wing into the satchel.

The distant sound of a rooster crowing could be heard from within the satchel.

"Where is it? Where is it?" The full length of the flamingo's wing was deep into the mouth of the satchel and the flamingos head was tilted in deep concentration as it tried to locate the missing object. Suddenly the flamingos face lit up as it had apparently located the mystery item.

"Catch!" It said as it tossed Noah a brown hard lump.

Without intending to, Noah caught the lump, his eyes were met by a very mundane sight indeed.

"It's a potato." Noah said as he held the potato up. "When it rings, answer it.

That's how we'll keep in touch."

"What do you—"

"No time. Now you," it pointed to Noah, "read out the instructions exactly. *Loudly*. And you," it pointed at Lottie "you follow the instructions *exactly*."

Noah took a deep breath and prepared himself to read the spindly handwriting again.

"Upon the arrival of the collector, the summonee will be enlisted by the enlister and summoner alike. The summonee must repeat the following 'From all angles of Wheyshaven, I do declare from Slothanary to Sealsfourth I shall commence.'."

Lottie paused and looked up at the flamingo. It gestured to her to hurry up.

"From all angles of Wheyshaven, I do declare from Slothanary to Fealsfourth I shall commence!" She breathed, making sure that each word was pronounced as clearly as possible.

"Exandor! Flipjibbot and tropston et concealia!" The flamingo boomed.

Bang. The sound echoed with such strength that Noah was knocked off his feet and hurtled across the room. There was a blinding flash of flight smoke suddenly billowed out from the shower. The smell of burned toast arose, choaking Noah as he spluttered heavily.

Chapter Tri

A Lost Summonee

The Depositorium is far beyond what you or I may come across on a cloudy Wednesday morning in early March, except for those people who travel to work using the train, then The Depositorium is exactly like a cloudy Wednesday morning in early March. Or June. Or a sunny day Thursday. Or rainy day in August. Or just about any day you choose to fall out of bed in the morning put on your work clothes and make your journey to work. The Depositorium is most likely to be familiar for those who take the train to work because The Depositorium is much like a train station. There's a busyness in The Depositorium in which bustling thems weave in and out each of each other, each one focused on their own business. Also, like a train station, thems at The Depositorium will bump and bounce of each other like pinballs in a pinball machine but all still determined to reach their destination with a sullen expression of daily life. But we digress.

The tinny call of the officer's announcement jingle boomed across The Depositorium. A sluggish and slimy voice made a general reminder to all thems who happened to be making a deposit or collecting a deposit at the time.

"We kindly ask customers to not spit on staff with acidic venom when they are being asked to show their tickets and remember, if your zerpiform is not announced at customs, your zerpiform will be incinerated instantly."

After the officer finished their announcement and the jingle played again. The green flamingo hurried around The Depositorium briskly trying to catch sight of Lottie.

"Goodtoads, where has it got to? All it had to do was repeat what its enlister said. Now there will be even less time." They moaned to themself as they stopped to tighten the buckle on their satchel.

"Count Shwangle the One-liest?" A metallic voice called, derailing the flamingos train of thought with a rude awakening.

"Yes?" Count Shwangle the One-liest replied as they eyed the tall blue vending machine with suspicion.

"Your collection?" The vending machine prompted with a twang of annoyance. Count Shwangle the One-liest immediately flushed a shade of turquoise at the notion and chose to avoid the glower from the little orange pixels on the vending machines displaypanel.

"Well, it's a funny story really," Count Shwangle the One-liest said forcing an obviously forced chuckle from their beak, "So I was collecting the summonee, for the summoner and…as I'm *sure* you're aware…I gave it very clear instructions to repeat what itsenlister said and well ... I sorta lost it…"

***

Plostangingio is a market, much like any farmers market you might choose (or bebribed) to visit. Except there aren't any boring things like tomatoes or fresh bread or anycarrots or beetroots that you might find in a farmers' market here. Oh no. Potangingio floats inside a glass bottle with no lid above the towns of Groggensworth, Oz and Dweslett andserves all sorts of unusual things you definitely wouldn't see at your local market. If it'sfloating above the towns, how does it not float away you might wonder? The thems of Wheyshaven are a very clever bunch and they chose to loop a thick rope of cramfardle furaround the neck of the jar over and over and over again until the bottle just bobs up and down in the same place, like a birthday balloon.

"Snottles! Get your juicy fat snottles! Only tri for a twolean amount!" The snottle merchant was calling to passersby when *crash*, the barrel of juicy fat snottles was completely smashedinto teeny-tiny smithereens by a very disorientated Lottie.

"Oi, watch it!" The disgruntled snottle merchant exclaimed as the wriggling pink and blue starred tentacles began to flip and flop around on the floor like a school of fish out of water.

"So-sorry!" Lottie stuttered as she tried to collect a handful of the oozing snottlesfrom the cobbled ground.

But as soon as she grabbed a handful, they all burst like a smallherd of water balloons and sent streaming goo (that smelt of the armpit of busy gruzzlebat) flying in every direction for a least twolean skentrools (for those who don't know the Wheyshaven measuring system, that's about the size of three giraffes as they eat calmly inthe savannah).

"Just go!" Growled the snottle merchant through gritted teeth as they wiped the goo from their thick glasses.

"Sorry!" Lottie apologised as she sprang to her feet and dashed away as quickly as she could.

Through the twists and turns of different alleys and stalls Lottie could not believe what she was seeing, hearing or indeed smelling.

There were stalls full of trupscorn, fustcrumples, wustpups. Words that weren't words, objects even less like anything Lottie had ever seen. As she began to slow down to ask for directions (or indeed ask where she was and where the nearest loo was), Lottie noticed a figure behind her. She hurried her speed. The figure hurried their pace too. Lottie tried to steal a glance behind her but there were too many thems to get a clear view of the thing following her. Without warning the them sped up and grabbed her shoulder. She screamed and tumbled to the floor with a loud *thrump*. She scrunched her eyes tight shut, as tight as they would go. *Leave me alone.* She thought.

"Lost?" A slow voice asked with a tone much like the calm a person might feel when they sit in a peaceful place alone and just watching nature roll around them. But Lottie wasn't convinced.

"No."

"Don't believe you." The calming voice answered as they leaned over and offered out an arm to help Lottie up. Lottie paused. As slowly as watching paint dry, Lottie opened her eyes. After a few seconds they fell into focus to find a giant tortoise (the size of an average red pillar post box) bending over her wearing an expression that feels only those who enjoy reading on a rainy day with a warm drink and cuddled under a blanket will understand.

"Excuse me?" Lottie blurted as she took the giant tortoise' arm and pulled herself up.

"I've never seen a creature like you before," the giant tortoise explained, "and certainly not in this shropnell."

Lottie flushed. She hadn't considered how *she* might be the strange one.

"Oh...yes...yes...I suppose I am a bit lost." She responded as she pretended to dust herself off.

"Melvyn." The tortoise answered as though it was an invite for introductions.

"Lottie." Lottie answered as she held out her hand with a small smile.

Melvyn looked down and it blankly then looked at Lottie as though she's performed a task that was beyond any reasoning. Lottie pulled her hand back as fast as she could and tried to paste a smile onto her face. There was a short time of awkward silence that certainly didn't feel like a short time as it seemed to have warped into a very long time.

"Where are you trying to get to?" Melvyn asked with air of genuine interest and huge tinge of nosiness that only busy-body neighbours will deeply understand.

Lottie, grateful for an opportunity to try and make sense of her surroundings took the question with great appreciation.

"I don't really know," she admitted feebly, "…a green flamingo just turned up and kept saying that Wheyshaven is in danger."

The expression on Melvyn's face dropped as quickly as a quiltdregg devours a yetsby.

"Oh no." They said, the calm tone turning into the kind of panic you get when you have lost your keys and you're outside in the pouring rain as your ice cream melts and all your pockets have been patted dozens of times but somehow still have the nerve to be empty.

"Oh no. Oh no. Oh no."

"What?" Lottie asked, her facing also dropping.

"Come with me." Melvyn said in a tone as serious as when you're told the cutting and ambiguous phrase *"we need to talk."*

The tortoise began to stride off with such a brisk pace it caught Lottie off guard.

***

Noah groaned slightly, holding his head which felt like it had been trampled on by a dazzle of zebras. The stentch of burned toast lingered in the air while the shower continued to run as merrily as anything, or anybody does when they are fulfilling their true purpose in life. *How did I end up here?* Noah wondered to himself as he gingerly stood up. Everything was hazy and distant, like a dream that slips away upon being awoken.

"Lottie?" Noah shouted. There was no response.

From the corner of this eye, Noah noticed something on the floor. His knees cracked loudly as he bent over the inspect the object more slowly. The purple book was laying open with the pages facing the floor.

Before Noah had time to pick it up from its disgruntled state, there was a phone ringing sound. Instantly, Noah patted his jeans pockets, but they were emptier than space. Rubbing his eyes with the heels of his hands, Noah tried to shake off the headache that was starting to take up tenancy. The ringing grew louder. Noah's eyes scanned the bathroom trying to locate the phone for noise. It's not until his eyes fell on the lumpy potato and that was shivering with each ring did Noah realise it was coming from that. His knees cracked again as his picked up the potato.

There was nothing extraordinary about this potato, in fact if you had not known it could ring you might very well have thought it was the most ordinary potato in the world, perhaps you might even think it was a little ugly. Noah checked for a button to stop the ringing but couldn't find one. In the meantime, the ringing grew louder and more aggressive as though it was feeling very hard done by, by Noah not being able to answer it. Noah accidently pressed one of the potatoes eyes (or better known as the sprouts of a potato) that the ringing stopped.

"Where is it?" A nasally voice demanded. The voice was distorted by the crackle of the radio effect so Noah could not place the voice but could sense the voice was familiar to him.

"Where's what?" Noah answered. The voice certainly was on the side of the headache that seemed to be hosting a very loud and very boisterous housewarming party in his skull.

"Where's the summonee?"

As though he had been struck by the god of memories a sudden cascade of images burst into his mind. A man in a fez. The purple book. A green flamingo. Lottie in the shower with the green flamingo.

"You mean Lottie?" Noah asked which such confusion that the headache that had been booming to the beats of heavy metal had now completely forgotten and replaced with confusion that was booming to the beats of heavy metal.

"Yes, yes. Where is it?" The flamingo persisted. "You *lost* her?

"Where is it?" The flamingo insisted, dodging the question with such grace that champion dodgeball players would have applauded.

"How am I meant to know?" Noah snapped with the sting of a lonely Lego brick being stood on with bare feet.

"The book!" The flamingo retorted with an equal measure of hostility. Noah muttered angrily to himself as he grabbed the book from the floor. "Stop muttering and help!" The flamingo jabbed.

Without any wonderment to how the book worked exactly, Noah's eyes scoured the growing paragraphs of poor penship.

"Err…she's in the market." Noah finally declared with the triumph of a someone who has just finished a marathon.

"*Which* market?" The flamingo asked, deflating the triumph like a needle to a balloon. "Plos…plos…" Noah struggled to decipher the letters in front of him.

"Plostangingio?" The pitchy crackled voice offered.

"Yes?" Noah confirmed with a huge hint of uncertainty.

"Bad. Very bad." The green flamingo more to themselves than Noah.

"She's with a giant tortoise called Melvyn apparently." Noah said, attempting to help the situation. But, like a thin roll of peeling tape against a thick crack in a wall, his efforts were unrewarded.

"I'll call you soon." The flamingo said as though Noah hadn't said anything at all. Then with a deafening *pop*, the potato stopped emitting any sort of crackly communication. Noah stared down at the potato. *Had that just happened?* As Noah's mind began to swirl with questions the shrill shriek of the doorbell screamed again. Noah hurtled out of the bathroom, stampeded down the stairs and tore the front door open.

Standing on his doorstep was a rather frail old lady. Her face was so deeply wrinkledface reminded Noah strongly of a raison or any other dried fruit that might make take yourfancy.

"I'm sorry dear," the elderly woman warbled softly, "I'm very lost. Can I come inand call my family so they can pick me up?"

On any normal day, Noah would have certainly offered help to a senior citizen who was a little confuddled without a second to hesitate. But *this* was not an ordinary day, so Noah hesitated for a second. As it happened, this turned out to be precisely the exact rightmove as while Noah was deciding on whether or not to help the woman in front of him, she was beginning to transform.

Chapter Quadstoff

Lighter Than a Freshly Baked Grogglesnatcher

When you think of a beast it's possible to think of something big and hairy with long sharp claws and teeth that can tear you apart from limb to limb such as a lion or a bear but that's nothing compared to a cramfardle. Oh no. A cramfardle is far sneakier. It has no claws, and its teeth resemble a few tic-tacs but the cramfardle does have a very unique quality that makes it far more dangerous than a lion or a bear. Cramfardles can sneeze snotty jelly that is so thick it fixes its prey to the spot leaving them unable to move. When a cramfardle has caught its prey, it will then jump up the prey's nose (no matter how tight, it'll always go up the nose) and then devour the prey's brain so quickly that the prey doesn't have time to realise their brain is being devoured. It should be noted that while cramfardles are hideous beasts and definitely should be avoided at all costs, they do in fact have a very strong mindset against rudeness. Should a cramfardle wish to pursue their prey, their manner is to be as polite as possible.

With a cramfardle on his doorstep, Noah had to escape. The cramfardle began to the wheeze the wheeze before you sneeze, so Noah smashed the door closed and bolted it shut. *Think. Think. Think.* Noah thought to himself as his brain became as blank as a new page of paper.

"The book!" He exclaimed. Pumping with more adrenaline than any adrenal medulla could produce, Noah flew up the stairs and into the bathroom. As the shower continued to cheerily run like one of those people that *like* running, Noah tore through the pages. It had to be somewhere.

The doorbell rang again, and a small boys voice could be heard distantly: "I've lost my mum; can you help me find her?"

Noah ignored the trap and examined the book as hastily as he possibly could. *Come on, come on.* The thought desperately. Meanwhile, the cramfardle had apparently come to the realisation that Noah wasn't falling for the disguise so instead chose a different approach:

"Please come out," the cramfardle pleaded with a patient tone that is heard by parents in restaurants when their child misbehaves. "I just want to devour your big tenderbrain. It won't hurt. In fact, it'll happen so quickly you won't know it has happened. Come on now, just let me in."

Noah continued to ignore the lure of the cramfardles offer when a lazy thought wondered into his mind as casual as a stroll in the sun in the park. The green flamingos voicesounded very distantly in his mind:

"If a cramfardle turns up remember, turn three times clockwise, half a turn anticlockwise and jump out with your arms out. It'll instantly explode."

Noah turned once clockwise. A second time. A third time. Then leaped into the airwith his arms stretched out so wide some might have thought him to be trying to fly like an eagle.

Bang. A sizzling sound blared through the air as Noah bent over holding his knees withhis hands and panting heavily. After catching his breath, he leaned into the shower and switched off the water. The shower instantly stopped but continued to tap droplets of waters as a protest against the joyous purpose being so rudely interrupted.

After tugging the shower curtain shut, Noah leaned against a cold tiled wall and closed his eyes. *Ring-ring, ring-ring.* The peace was shattered with the ring of the potato which was sat in the sink next to a large smudge of toothpaste. Noah jabbed the eye of the potato.

"What?" He sneered.

"Ahoy to you too." The green flamingo answered with enough sarcasm to fuel sarcasm city for tri woozes (or about six days).

"I nearly got killed by a--" Noah said so flatly than a crepe pancake would have looked like a balloon animal.

"No time, no time. What's happening with the summonee?"

***

Panting slightly, Lottie caught up to Melvyn. Their footsteps were lost in the sea of sounds as they dodged and dived to avoid other thems or miscellaneous objects that wereattached to stalls. Melvyn suddenly swerved off towards an alley, causing Lottie suddenly tocut in front of a browsing pletchley who was walking their pet zerpiform on a leash.

"Watch out!" The pletchley reeled.

"Sorry, sorry!" Lottie apologised. Unfortunately, the zerpiform got under Lottie's feet causing her to trip over it slightly. In surprise, the zerpiform vomited a small pebble to the ground then twitched its noses as though nothing had happened at all.

"Over here!" Melvyn's delicate tone floated through the commotion and Lottie hurried quickly towards where the giant tortoise was stood. After joining them, the tortoise sped down the alley, leaving Lottie had to jog to keep up.

"Where are we going?" Lottie asked as the alleyway quickly became dark and damp. She noticed sparkling pink goo with silvery glitter shining off a wall in the building to her side.

"To see The Great Oracle in the orchard of ewetrees and crabapples. Just back- yonder-upon-south of here. I might need to get some more fuel for the journey." Melvyn stopped so abruptly that Lottie didn't have time to veer away and bumped into the back of their boulder-like shell.

"Here we are." They continued, pointing towards a shape in the shadows.

Lottie strained her eyes into the darkness. There, leant up against the wall next to a sleeping rasting, was a tall unicycle. The legs of the unicycle seemed to be crooked with knots tried in the rusty metal, but it was without any doubt it was a unicycle. Lottie paused.

"I don't mean to be rude," she said as sensitively as could "but how are we both going to fit?"

The tortoise considered the problem for a moment, then with a small shimmy of the shell a tiny glass bottle fell from behind their tail. The bottle landed on the cobbles with an echoing clink which woke the sleeping rasting from its slumber. The rasting took a second to stick its tongue out at the pair to express its displeasure then scurried off to find another alley to settle. Unbothered by the rastings annoyance, Melvyn picked up the bottle and stretch out their arm. Lottie stepped back waving her hands in front of her and shaking her head vigorously.

"Oh no, no, no." She insisted, "This isn't some 'Alice Adventures in in Wonderland' potion that make me tiny, is it?'"

The giant tortoise shook their head.

"Oh no, Wonderland serums aren't really allowed in this region anymore since the Queen of Hearts fell out the with summoner. It all got very political. With this," they shook the tiny bottle, "you rub the oil, and it makes you lighter than a freshly baked grogglesnatcher."

Lottie tilted her head to the side as she considered this option. "So…it's a flying oil?"

"I suppose you could say that." Melvyn answered, shrugging.

Lottie reached for the bottle and tried to pull out the stiff cork. It didn't move. With all the energy could muster, she pulled the cork out with all her might, and it loosened. A short burst of air release like the sound of a fizzy drink being opened and Lottie removed the cork with ease. It was a strange oil. There seemed to be stripes of colour that layered up like oil and water mixed together.

"How much do I apply?" Lottie asked as she was about the tip the oil into her hand.

"Half a crazzler on the one-liest claw on the side towards Oxenwell and the same on the twelventeenth claw other side." Melvyn replied matter-of-factly.

Lottie stood looking at them blankly. Melvyn reached out a claw to help. Lottie reached out to give the bottle to them, but the bottle slipped out of her hand and shattered across the cobbled ground.

"I'm sorry, I'm sorry." Lottie leant over and began go collect the glass into a pile.

"Stop, stop!" Melvyn cried as they tried to pull Lottie up, but it was too late.

Lottie was beginning to rise up from the ground, gaining speed as she did so.

"Wha—what's happening?" She screamed as she ascended higher and higher.

Melvyn did another shell shimmy and a rope dropped to the ground. They seized it and tossed it towards Lottie. Lottie lunged for it, but the rope missed. Melvyn reigned the rope back in and launched it towards Lottie again.

"I…can't…reach…" She strained though gritted teeth.

***

After listening intently, Count Shwangle the One-liest, shook their head in utterdisbelief. The potatagram was pressed tightly to their ear and on the lowest volume possible.

"You've got to do something!" Noah commended with the force of tri pellymews.

"Okay, okay. Leave it with me." Count Shwangle the One-liest sighed.

"And if she comes to any harm. I'll personally--" Noah's growls were interrupted bythe fact that Count Shwangle the One-liest chose to hang up on the potatagram.

Of course, it smashed the bottle of oil. Of course, of course. Count Shwangle the One-liest thinked bitterly to themself as they dashed towards the elevationator. *Just the luck of the quazzlenaughts. Why this collection of any collection? I'll never get my twolean status at this rate.*

CountShwangle the One-liest thinked more grossumlessly as they clicked the button and waitedfor the elevationator doors to slide open.

As a side note, it should be recorded that an elevationator is extremely similar to an elevator that you might see in a shopping centre or in a skyscraper. Like an elevator, a them will proceed to follow these steps: press the button, step into a small space, avoid eye contact with others in the space, crumple themselves up small and stand in awkward silence while music in the background plays in an attempt to make the whole business feel more casual than it actually is. Unlike an elevatorthough and elevationator is not as smooth as an elevator and can travel in many directionsrather than just 'up' and 'down'. It can loop, swerve and zigzag in any direction it fancies andthere's nothing a them can do to from stopping the elevationator from choosing a randomorder to stop at.

Bing. The door slid open.

"The Depositorium!" The overhead voice announced brightly as Count Shwanglethe One-liest jumped inside and stabbed a button with a feather. The metal door snappedshut and the music filled the silence as they thinked deeply to themself.

Who knows what Gladysis going to say. They told me not to do it but no, I just had to be stubborn. They're going to be so disappointed.

"Cloud sixton!" The overhead voice announced brightly, snapping Count Shwangle the One-liest back to reality. The doors slid open and a large froglett Count Shwangle the One-liest vaguely knew from swishting club stepped into the elevationator. They beamed a large warm smile when Count Shwangle they saw Count Shwangle the One-liest.

"Long time, no swishting!" The large froglett chuckled as they pressed a button and took the space next to Count Shwangle the One-liest. Count Shwangle the One-liest smile a small polite smile and nodding slightly.

"How's your assessment going? I hope it's going well for you. That twolean will be yours soon!" The froglett boomed cheerily. It's hard to say if the froglett was ignoring Count.

Shwangle the One-liest's clear lack of interest in the small talk or whether the froglett simply loved small talk so much that they would press on until others would be forced to reply.

"Cloud ninquoz!" The overhead voice announced.

"This is me." Count Shwangle the One-liest smiled, relieved to have reason not to be forced into mindless small talk.

"Oh, okay." The froglett smiled with a sprinkle of disappointment in their voice, "Seeya!"

"Yeah, seeya." Count Shwangle the One-liest answered, shuffling out of the elevationator into the large room in front of them.

The doors had just clicked together with a dull snap and before Count Shwangle the One-liest could collect their thinks, a rasping booming voice screamed from across the room.

"Count Shwangle the One-liest!"

Here we go. Count Shwangle the One-liest thinked to themself.

Chapter Fivitt
A Griffin's Wisdom

A humongous (about the size of five hippopotamuses that are wallowing in mud) blob of oozing yellow sludge with tri eyes, quadstoff noses but no mouths slimed towards Count Shwangle the One-liest in a similar fashion to a snail or slug. This them is called a *bosseltri*, known for their grumplyish nature amongst the thems of Wheyshaven, they are not commonly considered good company. Unless you are a bosseltri yourself and then you consider yourself excellent company.

"Hey, boss," Count Shwangle the One-liest answered as they tried to stretch a stretch of a casual nature which actually turned out to be a stretch that pulled one of Count Shwangle the One-liest's wing muscles.

"How's it going?"

This bosseltri was a particularly grumplyish one and never had time for pleasantries, chit chat or jokes of any kind.

"Don't try to be all charming with me, One-liest." The giant oozing sludge blob retorted with a texture so scrapey that a box of sandpaper would have sounded positively smooth in comparison. "You know full well the protocol."

Count Shwangle the One-liests' hearts began to beat. *Did news travel that fast?*

"Ye-yes boss. Now, I know what you must be thinking. B-but I didn't know--" Count Shwangle the One-liest stammered, knotting their wings together in circles as a bead of sweat began to form on their brow.

"Didn't know? Didn't know?" The bosseltri thundered so loudly that the fluorescent lights flickered in fear. "I've told you goodtoads knows how many times. The gockles always need to be folded *in* when depositing a collection."

Count Shwangle the One-liest froze. *They don't know yet.*

"Now, make sure it doesn't happen again. I trust the summoner got the summonee?"

Count Shwangle the One-liest laughed nervously as they smiled a smile they hoped came across as a confident smile.

"Oh yes, yes."

"Good!" The bosseltri remarked as happily as any bosseltri can sound. As they began to slime away, Count Shwangle the One-liest let out a deep sigh and wiped the bead of sweat from their brow.

"See you later, boss." Count Shwangle the One-liest so longed the bosseltri with a little too much enthusiasm. They stopped and turned around very slowly, leaving a trail of yellow gloop on the floor.

"Mm-hmm. And the gockles goes *where*, when making a collection deposit?" The boss rasped, clearly trying to drive their point home like big lead mallet on a camping peg.

"They are always folded *in*." Count Shwangle said as studiously as they could.

Satisfied that the flamingo had now grasped the idea of the gockles, the bosseltri turned towards another unsuspecting worker and slimed towards them.

Count Shwangle the One-liest waited until their boss was far enough away then slipped towards a series of very mysterious looking doors that was generally ignored by the workers that worked in The Collection Office.
Now, which one for The Control Room? Count Shwangle the One-liest wondered to themselves as they folded their wings in deep think.

***

The market was growing tinier and tinier for Lottie at an increasingly rapid pace. "Help! Help!" She screamed, the panic in her rising as fast as she was rising into the cookie oat coloured sky. A few thems turned their heads to find the source of the noise, but upon locating that it, they simply shrugged off the matter in manner of such boredom it might have bordered completely mundane.

Lottie could just about make out Melvyn's boulder-like shell as she tried to swim towards it in the vain hope to lower herself towards them.

"Go to The Great Oracle!" Melvyn bellowed towards her.

"What?" She bellowed back. The wind was beginning to whip and trip and slip in away that made it hard to hear anything.

"Go to The Great Oracle!" Melvyn's voice tailed away as the wind completelyswallowed the voice.

How long am I going to go up for? Lottie wondered to herself. *Will I gradually descend, orshall I plummet to the ground like a stone?*

As Lottie began to imagine the various options in which her problem could result ina messy end, she heard the loud squawk of a bird echo through the wind. Suddenly, a pairof talons gripped onto her tightly and whizzed her yet higher into the air. Lottie shrieked as they climbed out of the bottle neck of Plostangingio and into the clouds.

Where is it taking me? She wondered to herself, hoping that she hadn't been capturedby an oversized vulture that would take her to its nest and gobble her up.

Where is it you wish to go? A warm voice asked her thought from within her head. Without taking a minute to consider why this new voice had popped into her head, she pondered the question with such deep thought that the floors in the deepest depths of theWollow Ocean could sooner be found.

"Well, Wheyshaven is in danger so I can't go home." She declared finally.

But where is it you wish to go? The voice in her head gently asked again.

"I want to go home." Lottie admitted.

Then home it is we go. The creature grasping Lottie suddenly swerved like a pilot changing course.

"But I can't go home," Lottie argued, impatiently with the voice.

And why is that? The voice asked with an air of genuine concern.

"Melvyn said something about a Great Oracle…and Wheyshaven is in danger…and…the summoner has summoned me…" Lottie clambered over her words totry and explain.

You can do whatever you wish to do, wherever you wish to do it, wherever you wish to do it. The voice answered with such disarming reasoning that Lottie was left blanker than a new notebook.

She considered this thought with great interest: now she *could* go home, did she *want* to go home? She wanted to go back to her home, to Noah, to the friends and family she loved. She wanted to see the boring blue sky and feel the drizzle of a cold Tuesday rain.

But in equal measure she wanted to make sure that Wheyshaven was safe from whatever it was it was in danger of. She knew she couldn't simply turn her back on the thems that could depend on her. The summoner had picked her for a reason and while she might not understand right now why, they obviously thought she was the right person for the job, and she couldn't let them down.

"I think..." Lottie murmured to herself.

Think and wish are different. What is it you wish? The voice pointed out with such needle like precision that Lottie couldn't help but feel slightly attacked. Lottie sighed deeply. She knew what she wanted.

"Take me to The Great Oracle." Lottie commanded firmly.

Instantly, the talons holding her gripped her a little tighter, and the creature above her veered off in a direction that somehow didn't make any sense to Lottie.

***

Noah snapped the book shut so ferociously that the air seemed to ripple out around him. Just as Noah was about to hurl the book out the bathroom window the potato began wail loudly. He stared at the potato, hoping there was a voicemail option that would allow him to hurl that out the window instead. Unfortunately, it didn't stop ringing and became angrier in its tone of ring.

"Yes?" Noah snapped at the potato after stabbing the potato's eye with the great force.

"Aren't you a delight on the potatagram." The familiar nasally voice remarked with equal measure of ice.

"What do you want flamingo?" Noah demanded, his temper becoming shorter thana baby yoplatt.

"My name is Count Shwangle the One-liest if you must know. A collector for thesummoner." The flamingo answered curtly.

"Not a very good one." Noah mumbled to himself as he wandered out of thebathroom and began to plod down the stairs. Each step was heavy and almost an effort.

"I heard that." Count Shwangle the One-liest replied, the crackly air not hiding a hintof their annoyance.

"What do you want?" Noah asked again, his voice trembling as he tried hard not to shout.

"I need the passcode the control room. What is it?" Count Shwangle briskly answered, apparently not remotely interested in what Noah had to say.

"You know I'm getting pretty tired--" Noah began as his temper boiled like a meat stew.

"No time. What is it?" Count Shwangle the One-liest insisted as their temper began to sizzle like a dynamite fuse.

"I dunno." Noah answered as he trudged into the kitchen. "It's in--"

"The book?"

"Yes. What is it?" Count Shwangle pressed, their voice becoming pitchier andpitchier as the conversation flowed.

"I dunno." Noah replied folding his arms and leaning on the doorframe.

"What do you mean, you don't know?" Count Shwangle the One-liest squawked.

"I mean, I don't know." Noah responded flatly. He wasn't going to let this flamingo just boss him about. Count Shwangle the One-liest sighed a deep heavily sigh and seemedto murmur sounds that made no sense.

"Where's the summonee?" They asked finally as though they had just had to keepthemselves from completely losing their temper.

"First of all," Noah growled through gritted teeth, "she has a name, and her name is Lottie. Second of all--"

Pop.

"Hello?" Noah asked quickly. No answer. *Rude.* He thought to himself.

As Noah was turning to go back upstairs that was a sound of a knocking on the window. Noah spun on his heal as though he had been stung by a jellywoop. There, stood outside on the patio, was Count Shwangle the One-liest.

"Oh, you gotta be kidding me." Noah mumbled to himself, his shoulders hunching over.

Chapter Sixton
Ewetrees

The potatagram is a device used by a few thems in Wheyshaven. Most are a little nervous of the gizmo as they have reservations about new technology but those who choose to use a potatagram find many uses for them. An interesting fact about the potatagram is that it's not just one particular type of potato that can collect sound frequencies. No. Just about any variety of potato can become a potatagram whether it's a Kennebec potato, King Edward potato, even a sweet potato (but these tend to make the frequencies a little tuney so it sounds like thems are singing a song rather than just normal chattering) can all be used for a potatagram. The only thing that a potatagram needs is to be is old enough to be sprouting the little eyes because it's through these that frequencies are picked up. Also, if you choose to boil your potatagram it will not have any adverse effects on your health although if you don't cook them for long enough, you may end up with a talking roast potato.

Although Noah had grown to dislike the device, seeing Count Shwangle the One-liest on his patio was far worse than a call on the potatagram.

"Go away!" Noah yelled as impatiently as a person who gets cut in front of in a queue.

"There's no time. Let me in!" The nasally bird argued pulling their wing up like a sleeve and pointing at the different watches.

"No." Noah called back as he tried to shoo them away with his arms.

The big green bird however was not scared away and instead unzipped their satchel and dove their wing deep inside as though looking for something that was deeper than physics could allow. A few seconds later, they pulled their wing out and seemed to be holding a small drink can that one might see in a shop for a fizzy drink. They snapped open the little can and in an instantly the green flamingo was in the kitchen.

"What?" Noah was so stunned his arms snapped to his sides like a soldier at attention.

"No time. Hurry." The flamingo strode towards the stairs, grabbing Noah by the wrist and dragging him behind them. As the flamingo's foot landed on the first step a rooster sounded from inside the satchel, distantly.

"Finally, some news!" The flamingo spat as they dropped Noah's hand and dug their wing into their satchel.

There was a distant clatter of saucepans clattering over from inside the satchel. The sound of the rooster got louder. The green bird pulled out their wing and stuck their beak into the satchel as though trying to peer in and get a better idea of the location of the crowing rooster. Upon spotting the place in which the rooster was, Count Shwangle the One-liest pulled out their beak from the satchel and stuck their wing in as far as it would go.

"Come *on.*" They muttered as they tugged and tugged. With feathers flying everywhere in a way that gave the impression a large pillow had burst, a rooster popped out of the satchel and cocked its head to the side peering up at Noah.

"No. Get rid of it. *Now.*" Noah snarled in a tone so snarly that Count Shwangle the One-liest sensed that this was not an opportunity for negotiation. The green bird snapped their fingers together with tri sharp clicks and the rooster had vanished leaving a small trail of feathers to delicately float to the floor in its place.

"Explain. Now." Noah struck sharply, folding his arms in a manner of such stubbornness that Count Shwangle the One-liest had to make a valiant effort not to tut and roll their eyes at him.

"Take a seat." They sighed.

***

Lottie and the creature holding her between the black shiny claws were beginning to descend through the clouds. While you might think they got as wet a wettlevice taking a shower in the rain, they didn't because it turns out that in Wheyshaven the clouds are silky smooth like handkerchiefs on your skin and dyer than the fluff from a tumble dryer. Lower and lower then went until they were out of the clouds completely.

"Bafflement. Utter bafflement." Lottie gasped as she gazed over a patchwork of patchwork patterned fields. There were green and yellow stiped fields next to fields of white and red polka dots. Some fields were plain and looked like they had a woollen texture, others had garish patterns that clashed with unfashionable colours.

As they began to get lower and lower towards the ground Lottie could make out a faint bleating sound. Her eyes scanned the sea of brightly coloured fields but could not find a single fluffablob in sight. The bleating grew louder as she as she noticed a thick collection of trees in the distant. Her eyes widened as they got closer and the bleating sounds to increase in volume until there was no denying what she was seeing.

As the creature dropped her gently only the dusty brown road, she could not resist but to take a closer look.

Sheep…on trees?" She thought to herself in utter puzzlement.

Ewetrees. A voice as comforting as being inside a blanket fort corrected her. She spun around to find an enormous griffin smiling back at her. *There are crabapples over there.* The griffin continued, tossing its head towards a collection of spiderly trees with glowing blue fruits that sprang up and down on the branches as though on a pogo stick.

As Lottie stepped towards the fruit trees, she noticed the griffin marching through the ewetrees.

It stopped and turned to her, its eagle eyes glittering: *This way to The Great Oracle.*

Lottie nodded then half jogged towards the creature, dirt crunching underneath her with each step. A long while passed in which the two walked together in each other's company without uttering a word or exchanging a passing thought. But Lottie found herself feeling at ease with the silence, it was refreshing and seemed to quench a thirst she didn't know she had been longing for. The orchard of ewetrees and crabapples began to thin, and a small clearing began to come into sight like a light at the end of a very long tunnel.

What should I ask them? Lottie suddenly thought as it was only now that it had occurred to her that she had no idea of exactly what help she needed.

Whatever you wish to ask. The griffin offered in an unhelpfully wise sounding but too vague manner that just left Lottie feeling more anxious than enlightened.

I suppose I could ask for directions. Or maybe why I'm here and what the summoner wants. She pondered to herself lightly as they stepped into the clearing of the orchard. Without warning, the griffin bowed its head in such a reverend manner it might have been thought it were in the company of royalty.

Ahoy, The Great Oracle.

***

Knowing that he might finally be getting some answers, Noah power walked towards the kitchen, and plonked himself down at the kitchen table. The now cold and long forgotten plates of sausage and mash sat before him like a calling ghost of a normality which he was starting to miss greatly. Count Shwangle the One-liest sauntered in with their wings and headed towards the kettle.

"What are you doing?" Noah quizzed them, alarmed. Count Shwangle the One-liest ignored him and began to explore the cupboards.

"Er...hello? What are you doing?" Noah said a little louder, waving his arms in the air.

"Making one-liest guzzle. Just need a pinch of salt and a plish of lump." The green flamingo's voice glided as they continued to check the cupboards. Upon finding a mug, they pour a heaped mountain of salt into it and began to utter sounds as though they were guzzling a large pitcher of water.

"Do you mind?" Noah said hotly, slamming his hands on the table which shuddered slightly.

Count Shwangle the One-liest stopped and sighed, bowing their head slightly in a manner which could easily be interpreted as the fact that they had had a very long day and just wanted a quick break. The green flamingo slowly turned towards Noah and leaned back against the counter, crossing their legs at their ankles.

"Goodtoads you're tiresome." They remarked at him as coldly as the airs swirling in the Moving Mountains.

"I'm warning you flamingo." Noah scowled back, stabbing his pointer finger at the bird.

"I told you. My name is Count Shwangle the One-liest--"

Before a stand-offish silence could commence, the doorbell range rudely. The twojust glowered at each other, refusing to back down.

"Aren't you going to answer that?" Count Shwangle the One-liest asked finally, breaking eye contact which gave Noah the secret feeling of immense satisfaction. Noah folded his arms and shook his head.

"Where's the book?" Count Shwangle asked slowly. Noah shrugged in such unbotherment that the green flamingo panic began to flash up.

"I told you to protect it at all costs. That means keeping it with you all the time!"

"Not until you tell me exactly what's going on." Noah gruffled, leaning back into hischair and shrugged again. The doorbell screeched again.

"Goodtoads this is tropplelighting," they sighed, "I already told you. Wheyshaven is in danger. There's no time. We need to hurry." The doorbell wailed for a third time.

"Will you answer that door?" Count Shwangle the One-liest burst out.

"Last time I did that, I was nearly killed." Noah replied flatly.

Count Shwangle the One-liest hurried towards the door, shaking their head vigorously. Noah jumped from his seat but before Noah could leap in front of them, theyhad pulled out their small cub and it clicked loudly. *Zap.*

"Ow! That'll bruise!" He whined, rubbing both his ears.

"No, it won't." The flamingo retorted from the hallway in a 'I-know-more-than-you-tone'.

"How do you know? You're just some stupid talking chicken with a stupid zapper. And a stupid potato. I should boil that potato." Noah grumbled to himself as he pulled over the freezer in search of ice for his ears.

"Will you stop muttering? The summonee could be in danger and you're just herewasting time poddlesnotching!"

Chapter Neves
The Great Oracle

The news rooster in Wheyshaven is much like a news reader you might see on the television or on the radio as it informs the Wheyshavenarians of news of the different regions from Wonderland and Oz to Oxenwell and Neverland to Plostangingio and Westlostashire and far, far beyond. Unlike the news you might be used to, this rooster has a voice which might remind you of a pushy salesperson in which it is a little too shouty and is a too enthusiastic about something that really shouldn't have that much enthusiasm.
The news rooster alarmed again from within Count Shwangle the One-liest's satchel. "Leaping lapnotches! Of *course!*" The flamingo said, smacking their wing to their head as though they had just solved a glaringly obvious riddle.

"What?" Noah asked, appearing in the doorframe in hope of a morsel of enlightenment.

"There's no time!" Count Shwangle the One-liest raced up the stairs and a faint echo of the shower began to drizzle down the stairs leaving Noah yet again, in the dark and strewing like on overly made cup of tea.

"Just keep the book safe." The nasally voice distantly called, "The summoner depends on it. When the potatagram rings, give me the code to The Control Room. It's the only way to save Wheyshaven."

Before Noah had time to protest, there was a *bang* so loud that the whole house shook a little and the smell of burned toast drifted down the stairs.

"Stupid summoner." Noah murmured to himself as he began to stomp up the stairs like a naughty child that had been sent to their room.

The bathroom was thick with steam as the doorbell rang again. Noah paused.

Should I answer it? He considered it lightly. *Hmmm, let me check something first...* Without taking a moment to pause about where the pang of intuition came from, Noah span clockwise. Then again. And again. He tuned half a turn anti-clockwise then finally jumped up with his arms stretched out as wide as he could make them.

Bang.

A sizzling sound carried through the air. *Ha, I knew I shouldn't have answered it.* Noah thought smugly to himself as his pulled open the large purple book and flicked through the pages quickly. The potatagram began to howl at him like a wolf to the moon.

"Code?" Count Shwangle the One-liest's voice crackled.

"Hold on, I'm just finding it." Noah answered, as his finger ran over the words carefully.

"Not like we are in a rush or anything." The flamingo tutted with such a tone that Noah could almost hear the bird rolling their eyes at him.

"Which control room?" Noah answered as he stumbled across pages that resembled some instructions of some variety. There was a long pause.

"What do you mean, *which* control room? There's only one-liest." Count Shwangle asked, their voice seeping with suspicion.

Noah watched as the instructions began to split and grow into new instructions. The new instructions would then split themselves into more instructions in a way that would make any person who suffered motion sickness feel very queasy indeed.

"No, there's one…two…three… They're just growing!" Noah began to count but the rate in which the instructions were changing was so fast he just could not keep up. A heavy sigh crackled through the potatagram.

***

The Great Oracle is a thems might be considered a them of an interesting nature or perhaps a terrible bore depending on one's view of what is interesting. They live in a structure that strongly resembles a giant thimble with a long turret-like chimney poking out the side. The Great Oracle themselves have never been sighted to be stood up but always sat down with their legs crossed like a guru monk and always floating about quadstoff measures from the ground. They have a small trunk with bat-like ears that twitch from side to side occasionally. The Great Oracles eyes seemed to bulge out slightly, like a rubber toy that has been squashed. Their skin was heather lavender blend which glints with a shine that almost gives the them a glittery effect.

Lottie stared at The Great Oracle, noticing that they had mophead on their head in a way that almost resembled hair (if you didn't notice the plastic socket protruding from the mophead, you might have been forgiving for mistaking it for the hair of The Great Oracles and not a mophead at all).

The Great Oracle, I'd like you to meet… The griffin telepathized with a voice as humble as an apple crumble. There was a long pause.

"Meet?" The Great Oracle demanded in a deep but uncomfortably fast tempo.

The griffin turned it head towards Lottie then cocked its head to the side as though waiting for her to jump in an introduce herself.

"L-Lottie." Lottie stammered, a little unsure if it was in fact her name.

The Great Oracle, I'd like you to meet Lottie, summonee.

"Summonee?" The Great Oracle asked, as though they were only able to repeat the ends of the griffin's sentence.

Apparently so. The griffin telepathized again, bowing their head again.

"Great Oracle helps not summonee." The Great Oracle declared as though they were a judge in a court.

"Excuse me?" Lottie gasped as though she had been stung by a wasp.

"Great Oracle excuses summonee, they do." The Great Oracle answered in a bored tone that suggested they really did have more important things to attend to and this was a colossal waste of energy.

"You're…you're not going to help?" Lottie stuttered, completely bewildered that she hadn't considered that The Great Oracle might not be of any assistance at all.

"Great Oracle is in agreement with summonee." The Great Oracle nodded with the eagerness of a hungry person seeing a plateful of food heading towards them.

"But…*why?* I've come all this way to see you." Lottie asked, stamping her foot on the ground with such force that a small cloud of dirt fluttered up and finally settled.

"Great Oracle interested they are not." The Great Oracle glumped as they inspected their fingernails for dirt.

"Wheyshaven is in danger. That's why I've been summoned." Lottie pleaded desperately.

"Great Oracle poses tri questions to summonee they do. Should summonee question right-so one-liest, Great Oracle helps they will." The Great Oracle proclaimed as they continued to inspect their fingernails for dirt.

"So, I've just got to answer one question right…and you'll help?" Lottie asked with more hope in her voice than she was hoping to let on.

"Great Oracle is in agreement with summonee." The Great Oracle nodded as they began to gnaw at a jagged fingernail.

After spitting out the fingernail jagee (which went a surprising distance) The Great Oracle cleared their throat and asked in a formal tone: "Question one-liest: Enlister for you be?"

Lottie stared at them. *What on Earth?* Her mind was completely blank to the question

"I'm sorry?" Lottie spluttered as she tried to make sense of the riddle in the hope The Great Oracle would repeat the problem in a slower tempo in order for her to grasp more easily.

"Great Oracle must say no-so to summonee. Correct answer: Noah." The Great Oracle answered briskly as they attempted to fit a toe to their mouth as though they were going to file their toenails with their teeth.

This answer was like a finishing punch in a boxing match that blew the wind right out of Lottie's stomach.

"Noah…How?" She whispered, her eyes welling up with tears so plump you could almost pluck them from her eye and make a jam out of them.

"Question two lean: Where of enlister be where the by?" The Great Oracle continued as they struggle to get their toe to their mouth and clearly had no interest in the events that were unfolding around them.

"I don't understand! What--" A fat tear dropped from her eye and plopped into the dirt like a single drop of rain in a desert.

"Great Oracle must say no-so to summonee. Correct answer: Showerbowl."

The Great Oracle answered as they strained with their narrowing their eyes against the struggle to fit their biggest to their mouth.

"Showerbowl? Where's that? Is he okay--" Lottie had a tidal wave of questions about Noah and his involvement in all of this.

"Question tri: The summoner summoned the summonee for why?"

The Great Oracle asked as they lowered their foot down back into the folded position in a way to suggested they had given up trying to nibble at their toenails. They folded their arms in agrump and glowered at Lottie.

"I don't *know*! That's why--" Lottie wailed, her eyes becoming dangerously close to opening a tap of uncontrollable tears.

"Great Oracle must say right-so to summonee."

***

Count Shwangle the One-liest held their potatagram close their ear as they surveyed the doors in front of them. One was large and wooden with an intricate looking knocker on the front, one was about the height of a meerkat and as thin as a candle with a metallic finish and a third looked like it belonged to a cupboard under the stairs. As Count Shwangle the One-liest peered down the hall, they noticed doors of all shapes and sizes but was sure that the door to The Control Room was one-liest of the tri they stood before. *Think. Think. Think.* They thought as they rattled their thinks for a marble of ideas.

"Reset the control settings?" They hissed into the potatagram.

"What control settings?" Noah's voice crackled through glumply.

Goodtoads give me strength. Count Shwangle the One-liest thought to themself as they inhaled deeply.

"At the back. Hurry!" They answered as their eyes darted around to ensure they weren't drawing attention to themselves. There was a faint crackle of paper as Noah could be heard flicking to the back of the book.
"Err...oh 'To reset the control settings you must do the following. 1) Locate

the plock at a diagonal to the frats... 2) Cranch—'" Noah's voice read in an almost robotic tone.

"Hold on, I'm just finding the plock." Count Shwangle the One-liest reached towards a small control panel covered in an array of buttons that wizzed and bizzed and glowed and woawed in their own way. A small toggle that resembled a light switch but turnedlike a second hand on a clock could be found. "There we go."

"2) Cranch the plock until dropped flat."

Count Shwangle the One-liest pushed small toggle down and it squeaked like a smallmouse and tried to wriggle out from under the flamingo's wing. After a few seconds, thetoggle gave up and became as limp as a washed lettuce aloud.

"Next." Count Shwangle barked quietly into the potatagram.

"3) With the dropped plock state your name and utter 'Reset controls.'." Noah read.

"Count Shwangle the One-liest. Reset Controls." The bird said with a touch too much uncertainty to convince anyone that they knew what they were doing.

"Access granted." A voice announced.

"What's the code for the control room?" Count Shwangle asked breathlessly, gripping the potatagram so tightly their knuckles were beginning to ache.

"Er…To access the control room, authorized thems must type in thems unique code given to authorized personnel." Noah read, his voice stumbling slightly as he was trying to understand the etchings on the paper in front of him. Count Shwangle the One-liest's stomach dropped into the pits of the floor and their face drained from emerald to olive.

"Oh crucklejuts. I don't have one." They muttered to themselves.

Chapter Ate
Toolio of Imangery

Noah stood in the steaming bathroom seething so much it might have been thought that he'd made the bathroom steam, not the shower.

"What do you mean, you don't--"

Pop. The potatagram went silent. Noah hurled the potato across the room and smashing into the mirror with a heavy smack and landed on the floor with a thud. The mirror toppled from side to side trying to keep its balance on the nail it clung to.

"I can see where Count Shwangle the One-liest is coming from." A shrill voice piped up.

Noah span around. No one. He Span around the other way. Still no one.

"Ahoy! Down here." A little tinkle of a rattling sound split the air. "Diddly at your service, Diddly Brush."

Noah stepped towards the sink to find his worn red toothbrush covered in toothpaste stains was quivering side to side and tapping on the murky glass in which it was stood.

"But...you're a *toothbrush*." Noah spluttered.

"No need for that," Diddly Brush answered with a sulky twist in their voice, "I'm a them just like you."

Noah took a step back and rubbed his eyes, shaking his head.

"I need to get some air," he mumbled to himself, "I'm talking to a toothbrush."

"I'm starting to see why the collector is getting annoyed with you. Especially witheverything that's going on." The toothbrush sleeked, turning their bristles away from Noahin a way that showed that it would have folded its arms too if it had any to fold.

"What *is* going on?" Noah shouted, flapping his arms around like he was miming being an aeroplane. "All I wanted to do was to have a nice evening with Lottie but-""Yes, yes, yes. It's all hard being the enlister to a summonee." Diddly Brush interrupted sourly.

"A what?"

"You really need to read the manual." Diddly Brush sighed as they turned their bristles back towards Noah.

"What manual?" Noah asked suspiciously.

"The Wheyshaven Enlister Manual, *obviously*." The toothbrush moved its head rigidly back and forth as though shaking their head. "It's almost like you just stumbled into all ofthis."

"I *did* just stumble into all of this." Noah burst out, his nostrils flaring so open thata cramfardle would have jumped up his nose with no problem at all.

The toothbrush began to clink and clack against the glass in shock.

"You mean to tell me that you just happened across the Adventures of Wheyshavenand enlisted the summonee without knowing what you're doing?" Diddly Brush squealed.

"What are you talking about?" Noah thundered, spitting a few drops of spittle in his temper.

"Goodtoads, Wheyshaven really is in danger. You need to get that manual fast." Diddly Brush insisted, doing well not to retaliate at Noah's outburst but focusing on theproblem at hand. Noah paused.

"Where do I get that?" He asked, his voice lowering slowly as he regained control ofhis tantrum.

"Now you're being deliberately rolassum." The toothbrush tutted. "The Emporiumof the Lost and Found will be a good place to start."

***

With a swish of their arms, and a clap on their ears, The Great Oracle fabricated a small object out of thin air. It floated towards Lottie with a slightly apricot glow-tinge around it. Lottie reached for the object, and it settled into her hand and seemed to snuggle into her fist like one does when they snuggle into a bed.

"Great Oracle offers this to summonee they do." The Great Oracle remarked with a small bow of welcome.

Lottie opened her first to inspect the object. It was a black pen. When you think of a pen that is being offered by an almost deity-like them, one might assume the pen was expensive looking and elaborate like a fountainpen or a quill. This however, the pen in her fist looked like a corporate pen that one might steal from work or nab when they attend a conference that they were forced to go to. Lottie's face sank with disappointment.

"A pen?" She said, trying her best to sound enthused and failing miserably.

"Great Oracle knows not what a pen is, but Great Oracle offers summonee Toolio of Imagery." The Great Oracle learned forward and completed a small summersault in excitement for the gift they had given.

A prize of great honour. The griffin telepathized to Lottie. She looked at the creature and its eyes shone with the calm of a spring day. She nodded reluctantly, knowing she ought to be grateful for any sort of help.

"Er…thank you…" She smiled at The Great Oracle. "How does it work?"

The Great Oracle's face dropped and became distant and almost stern as though she has posed a great philosophical question of the universe.

"Great Oracle says they cannot tell precisely. Great Oracle can say that Toolio of Imangery is limited to summonee powers alone so limitless it can be." The Great Oracle chortled again and did another summersault while still sat with their legs crossed.

What does that mean? Lottie wondered as she inspected the pen more closely.

"Great Oracle can say a clickity-click and the powers are unlocksworth!" The Great Oracle cackled with delight.

Lottie's eyes snapped up at The Great Oracle, then down at the pen. With her thumb, Lottie reached for the top of the pen. The Great Oracle leaned in, grinning. The griffin's eyes widened. Lottie held her breath.

Click. The pen clicked open. There was a sound like a lightning strike and Lottie landed somewhere she certainly wasn't before.

Plates, bowls, pots, and pans shattered onto the floor, making quite an announcement of her presence. As she clambered to her feet she spun round looking desperately in every direction.

"Oi, who are you?" A young man asked, jumping from the leather chair next to a raging fire.

"Where…where am I?" Lottie asked as she noticed a darkening sky from a small window. The room felt small and cosy. The rich musty warmth of smoke was inviting and lulled Lottie to slow down and relax.

"In my cabin." The young man answered, folding his arms, and tapping his foot on the rug impatiently.

"Lottie…Summonee…I--" Lottie's words were tumbling out like a laundry in a washing machine.

The young man's face lifted into a cheery grin.

"Ah yes. The summoner told Tinkerbell you might be stopping by. I suppose the High Council will want to speak with you."

***

The rooster sounded from Count Shwangle the One-liest's satchel. They quickly unzipped it and after a short effort to locate and pull out the plump creature it plopped out in front of them.

"Rooster, rooster of the mooster, upon what's agoing on?" Count Shwangle the One-liest recited as though they were talking to a magic mirror.

A news jingle blared and Count Shwangle the One-liest jumped in shock at the blaring volume the rooster was making. A few colleagues looked at them and glared disapprovingly. As though burning from fire, Count Shwangle the One-liest grabbed the roosters and knocked the wattle (the dangly bit underneath the roosters chin) down until the rooster was in a hushed voice.

"The weather in--" The rooster said in its television presenter type voice.

"Next." Count Shwangle the One-liest hissed.

"In sports, the--"
"Next."

"The Queen of Hearts continues to demand more time--""Next." Count Shwangle muttered breathlessly.

"Lexivarians--"

"Next."

"Dorothy the--"

"Save for later and next." The rooster glintered a sound like a document being saved to a computer.

"Search 'summonee'." Count Shwangle the One-liest whispered. A few seconds passed as the rooster seemed to need time to search and buffer this request.

"Missing summonee not deposited--" The rooster trumpeted out like a soloist in a choir.

"Open!" Count Shwangle the One-liest instructed, knocking the wattle down as not to be heard.

"The summonee, known as Lottie, has not been signed for by the summoner..." The new rooster roared out to the whole office.

"Count Shwangle the One-liest!" A voice echoed so loudly the lights flickered and quivered in fright again. Squenching, squishing, sliming sounds oozed from around the corner and Count Shwangle the One-liest's jaw dropped.

"Close!" They muttered to the rooster. As quickly as they could, the flamingo tossed the rooster into their satchel and zipped it up leaving a small cluster of feathers knotted at the top.

"Oh, hey boss!" Count Shwangle the One-liest greeted the bosseltri with a small wave that tried to cover up any suspicious behaviour as stealthily as a bull completing a diamond heist.

"The summonee *hasn't* been deposited? You told me it had." The raspy voice exclaimed with ice the strength of sixton measured icicles on the Moving Mountains.

"Well…yes, yes I did but--" Count Shwangle the One-liest's words began to twistand dance like a gymnast as a competition.

"No excuses. Assessment failed." The bosseltri glowered but with an unquestionableglint of pleasure to the event.

"But boss--" They protested, falling to their knees, tears bubbling up. Count Shwangle the One-liest stared up at the bosseltri hoping their desperation would change theirmind. *This can't be happening.* They thought to themselves. *It just can't be happening.*

"Thank your lucky quazzlenaughts that you still have a job," the bosseltri sourly skimpered with an air of distain. They were right of course, a collector who did not deposita summonee to the summoner could lose their job and therefore failing the twolean assessment could be considered almost merciful of the bosseltri.

"Now, where *is* the summonee?" The bosseltri wrangled as all their eyes narrowedwith overlish suspicion and somehow glistened greedily at the misery of the One-liest's shortfall.

"I…I…I don't know." The green flamingo sniffed quietly as they hung their headlike a disappointment-cherry hangs from a disappointment-cherry tree.

As one might imagine, the disappointment-cheery is not a fruit one chooses to eatfor celebrations of happy events such as birthdays or Saturdays but chewed upon when one is feeling sorry for themselves and want to wallow in a deep pit of their own self-misery (it should be noted that the disappointment-cherries are most commonly consumed on a Sunday night at approximately twolean past the ate). Unlike what you might imagine, they don't taste like cherries at all but taste a lot more like a mango-raspberry cross and are only called 'cherries' because the them that stumbled across the fruit decided they liked the soundof the word 'cherry'.

Chapter Enino
A Pan Special

The whole office stared at Count Shwangle the One-liest as they passed, with their head hanging and shoulders hunched over like a them in the deepest shame. Colleagues whispered and pointed at them as they passed. The bosseltri slimed next to them, snorting heavily, and leaving a thick creamy sludge of a trail behind them. The two thems steered into a room and the bosseltri knocked down the blinds so no nosy nositrons could nosy in.

"What are you going to do now then?" The bosseltri rasped as Count Shwangle the One-liest sank into a chair.

"Well…I was hoping to get into The Control Room…" The flamingo explained with a glimmer of hope in their voice, "I was going to trackle the summonee through the gumstrops to pinpoint the summonee and…and then do a long distance deposit using the noxfound--"

The bosseltri roared with laughter and Count Shwangle the One-liest fell back into their chair.

"With what code?" The bosseltri jeered. "You need to be Tensnoot status for that and you've not passed your Twolean assessment. I'm taking you off the case and putting Count Robsagonn the Tensnoot--"

Count Shwangle the One-liest jumped up from their seat so quickly the chair tipped back and landed on the floor with a thudder.

"No, no. Please boss. Let me stay on the case…I really want to do it. Please…" Count Shwangle the One-liest begged and grovelled with such conviction that even the grumpliest bosseltri would have found it hard to resist. The bosseltri sighed a sigh you sigh when knew you are going to regret a choice but do it anyway.

"Fine. You can shadow the Tensnoot. But if you put so much as one of your little green feathers out of line you won't be on the case anymore. Understand?"

"Thank you, thank you. I won't let you down." Count Shwangle the One-liest nodded enthusiastically.

"We shall see about that." The bosseltri glowered. "You're treading on very broken shrapgons, One-liest. Very broken shrapgons."

Count Shwangle the One-liest gulped. This wasn't quite the encouragement and mentorship that they has been hoping for.

"Count Robsagonn the Tensnoot?" The bosseltri chimed into thin air.

Out of nowhere a tall willowy white rabbit popped up wearing a brown waistcoat. A chain slung outside the pocket as a statement to the fact that they owned a pocket watch,and their face was long and sour looking as though they always tasted lemons.

"Yes boss?" Count Robsagonn the Tensnoot chimed in a voice so clammy one couldalmost feel the sycophant slime dribbling off them like sweat.

Show off. Count Shwangle the One-liest thought to themself. It's hard to tell if CountShwangle the One-liest was unimpressed with this trick because they were unable to do itthemselves for it was an exceptionally challenging skill to complete without aid or because they were genuinely unimpressed. It is generally agreed the first, but the latter is entirelyplausible.

"You are in charge of the case that One-liest just failed." The bosseltri instructed the white rabbit.

The rabbits face crumpled into an expression of what could almost pass as sympathyto those who did not know the them well.

"Oh no, I'm so sorry--" Count Robsagonn the Tensnoot burbled in a manner thatmade Count Shwangle the One-liest's feathers shrivel up and crawl with unease.

"Don't be. Just find the summonee, deposit it to the summoner and then we can get on with things." The bosseltri drawled in their raspy tone.

"Yes, boss. Of course, boss. Whatever you say, boss." Count Robsagonn grundledbowing their head slightly.

"Good!" The bosseltri wheezed as they opened the door and oozed out with sludgingly slow ease. Count Robsagonn the Tensnoot and Count Shwangle the One-liest followed behind them towards the corridor of mysterious doors.

"So, failed your twolean then? I remember when I took the assessment--" Count Robsagonn the Tensnoot chuckled with glee.
.
"Oh, shut up." Count Shwangle the One-liest interrupted with a streak of agitation that they couldn't quite hide.

Count Robsagonn the Tensnoot stopped dead then folded their arms and looking the green flamingo up and down as though they were examining a vaguely interesting artpiece.

"Very well…" Count Robsagonn the Tensnoot glided. "Grab me a glug with a pinch of salt and let the *real* collectors do the work."

"I *am* a real--"

Count Robsagonn the Tensnoot waved their arms in interruption, forcing Count Shwangle the One-liest to faulter in their argument.

"Oh, and if you could just not talk to me while I work, that would be great." Count Robsagonn smiled a jeery grin and wandered towards the door that looked like it belonged to a cupboard under the stairs.

"But it's *my* case." Count Shwangle the One-liest whined like a small child that doesn't get their way as they followed the white rabbit.

"Not anymore. Now, where's that glug? Or do you want to be completely off this case?" The white rabbit retorted as they inputted a series on squirls into the control panel.

"Fine." Count Shwangle answered, folding their arms, and tossing the white rabbit the filthiest look they could muster.

"Good. And remember, a pinch of salt in the glug." Count Robsagonn the Tensnoot answered distractedly.

Count Shwangle turned towards the kitchen, shaking their head furiously.

"Access granted." A voice announced.
Count Shwangle the One-liest stopped dead. They spun around and raced up

to the white rabbit.

"Can I at least watch in The Control room first?" The flamingo pleaded pushing their face as close to the white rabbits as possible in a way that the white rabbit was forced to move their head away to regain any sense of personal space.

One-liests. The white rabbit thought to themself bitterly. *Just my luck to land with a failed twolean.*

"Fine. But you best bring me some juicy fat snottles with that glug." The white rabbit agreed through gritted teeth.

The two thems clambered into the door that looked like it was made for a cupboard under the stairs and Count Shwangle the One-liest was mesmerised. There were large portals in every direction. Each spinning and bustling into each other like a crowd on a street. For those of you who are not familiar with a portal of Wheyshaven, these are pineapple shaped holes that resemble a black hole somewhat.

"Whoa...What *is* all this?" Count Shwangle the One-liest asked.

"Just some average monitoring." Count Robsagonn the Tensnoot answered as casually as if Count Shwangle the One-liest had asked them what day of the week it was.

"Code?" They continued as they slumped into an office chair and pulled out a typewriter from the side of the chair. Count Shwangle the One-liest tore their eyes way from the dodging portals and tried to focus. Somehow the stream of portals had drained their memory of the task at hand.

"#L95-@N96-AOWH--" Stumbled the green flamingo, racking their head hard with their wing as a means to direct their attention on the white rabbit's r equest.

Count Robsagonn the Tensnoot clattered the string into the typewriter and their eyes narrowed. Nothing with the portals seemed to change. None were filtered out. None were outlined in any different colours. Everything continued in its chaotically business-like manner. As Count Robsagonn the Tensnoot began to re-type the string into the typewriter the rooster began to alarm rudely.

"Will you shut that thing off?" Count Robsagonn the Tensnoot snapped.

"Sorry, sorry." Count Shwangle the One-liest apologised as they opened their satchel and dumped up the rooster.

"Rooster, rooster of the mooster, upon what's agoing on?" Count Shwangle the One-liest recited quickly, knowing the mute button had to unlocked from the inside. The news jingle jangled loudly and Count Robsagonn the Tensnoot sniffed in equal measure of noisiness to highlight their disapproval.

"Missing summonee has been sighted..." The rooster exclaimed.

***

Lottie stared at the young man in front of her. His fair hair was effortlessly messy in a charmingly deliberate way. His eyes glittered, gleamed and almost danced with youthful mischief.

"Tinkerbell...So you're..."

"Peter. Nice to meet you." He tipped his head in a greeting.

"Wow...I thought..." Lottie gazed over the young man's face. It wasn't quite the boyish figure she'd imagined but somehow this fitted him well. Grey clouds began to rumble like a hungry stomach and Peter's eyes snapped towards the window like a deer that hears a snapping twig in a forest.

"I guess we'll have to wait." He murmured to himself in thought.

"What for?" Lottie blurted out. She smacked her hands to her mouth in surprise then shook her head as though to apologise profusely.

"It's not safe to fly in this weather." Peter explained and he peered more closely at the rain through the window that seemed to bounce of the roof of the cabin.

"You can use Wendy's bunk and we will fly to the High Council in tomorrow. Tinkerbell?"

A small light glittered and shone from behind a bottle. *Wow.* Lottie thought to herself.

"Oh, there you are." Peter smiled at the glittering light. The small like tinkled a tinkle that only the feeling of a dark room filled with fairy lights can make you feel.

"Tinkerbell. Tell the summoner I've got the summonee and we will meet the High Council tomorrow."

The glistening light tinkled again, moving lightly in circles to make its point. Peters' eyes narrowed like a student listening carefully to a teacher.

"Yes, yes. Of course, I'll record it for you."

The shining light tinkled again the whizzed away like a racing car.
Peter smiled at Lottie and offered her the rocking chair opposite the leather chair in the range of the fire. Lottie found herself moving towards the chair and delicately taking the place.

"Hungry?" Peter asked, his grey-blue eyes twinkling as brightly as the moon on a clear night.

Lottie nodded, somehow unable to find her words.

"What are you in the mood for? Pan's special?" Peter beamed. "A lot of devour, a couple of chomps, a sprinkling of snap and a touch of zestful. The zestful just adds a little kick."

Lottie, still unable to find her words, simply nodded with a grin. Peter sat down in the leather armchair and picked up the guitar that was balanced against the arm of the chair.

"A day, a night of pure cunfright, Pan calls for your delights. With lexi and grunt Pan does penunt a grime of fun and grash A trumplet, a grumplet, et gonnuplett. Shoo-kanoo." Peter sang with a melody enchanting Lottie felt herself being lulled into a state of comfort she hadn't felt in a very long time.

***

Noah stood with his arms crossed, frowning a frown that could probably frown its own frowns.

"I don't know where--" A distant memory flashed in the corners of his mind: a battered shop sign with peeling paint.

"Just get the manual. Call Count Shwangle the One-liest and save

Wheyshaven."Diddly Brush screeched from the glass.

Noah snapped back the bathroom with a heavy bump.

"But why is Wheyshaven in danger? Why is it us that has to save it?" Noah streamed the questions that had been bubbling like the bath inside of him.

"Wow, you really are rolassum." Diddly Brush sighed, tipped their bristles down slightly. "You don't pay attention at all, do you?"

Noah glowered at the toothbrush and wondered if he should cover it in toothpaste and brush his teeth with it just to make a point.

"To what?" He scowled, deciding that the toothbrush would still give him a hard time even if he did choose to brush his teeth. "All I've been told is Wheyshaven is in danger."

"And…" Diddly Brush said slowly like a patient teacher helping a child connect the dots.

"And what?" Noah glowered.

"There's no time." The toothbrush sighed.

"Yes, yes. I know it's urgent!" Noah shouted, fed up with the circular arguments of those in the know. "But I don't know *why*."

"No…" Diddly said in a gentle soothing tone. "*Think* about it…"

Noah paused. His eyes widened like the large platters at a fancy dinner. He dashed towards the book and tore it open. Racing quickly through the pages his mind began to ping clues together like a detective who had just been given a hot lead. Voices and visions began to rise in his mind like springs that had been held down too long and had now been released with exceptional power:

"To see the Great Oracle in the Orchard of ewetrees and crabapples. Just back- yonder-upon-south of here. I might need to get some more fuel for the journey. Here we are."

"Goodtoads this is tropplelighting. I already told you. Wheyshaven is in danger. There's no time. We need to hurry."

"The Queen of Hearts continues to demand for more time…" Noah snapped the book shut, his mind swimming and spinning.

"It's not a figure of speech." Noah yelled. "There's no time. Literally. That's why Wheyshaven is in danger. Because time is...some sort of fuel?"

"Finally!" Diddly Brush sighed as though the hardest part was over.

Chapter Tensnoot
A Broken Protocol

You might be wondering how time might be used as a fuel for the Wheyshavenarians to use. After all it's a concept we used to measure the rotations around the Sun. However, Wheyshavenarians found they could mine time in clumps much like a lump of gold or a diamond can be mined. A lump of time in its rawest form looks a lot like a chicken's egg in size, wight and colour but rattles like a board game with many pieces. These rattling pieces are in fact *possibilities*. Whether it's a possibility of the future or a wonderment of "what if" from the past, time is made up many rattlelites of possibilities. It's through the possibilities of time that it become a fuel source that can be used to be a sp powerful that it made go between towns or regions positively effortless. The commodity became so popular thems began to give their loved ones 'the gift of time' which is a time mine, while others pumped it straight into their vehicles like we might pump petrol, diesel or electricity into our cars. With his newfound insight, Noah tore into the little stuffy antique shop in which started the whole debacle. The bell was smashed into and rang loudly, more in pain of the force in which Noah had pushed into the door rather than to announce his arrival.

"Where are you?" Noah demanded, head spinning in every direction to find the shop keeper.

"Where are you?" He demanded again, raising his voice which almost trembled with emotion.

"Yes?" The shop keeper answered, appearing again from seemingly nowhere and settling behind the shop counter, holding a chipped teacup and saucer on his hand.

Noah raced towards him, grabbed him by the shoulders and shook him so hard, the fez dropped off the shop-keepers head and the hot drink in the teacup spilled onto the saucer. Noah's eyes were wide and bulging.

"*Wheyshaven Enlister Manual.* Need. Now." Noah whispered so fast he seemed almost frenzied.

"I'm sorry, I don't have it." The shop keeper replied, sinking away from Noah's faceand trying to remove himself from the grip he was trapped in.

"What? Where is it?" Noah yelled, spitting all over the shop keeper's cheek.

"I sold it not long after you left." The shop keeper answered. Noah's heart dropped. As though the shop keeper was made a splintering hot coal, Noah let go of the him and began to pace around the shop, shaking his head.

"Who was it, do you know them?" Noah paused, serving the question towards theshop keeper like a tennis player in a finals match.

"It doesn't seem like you've quite got a handle on things." The shop keeper playedback, with a disarmingly coy smile. Noah stared at the shop keeper. *What did he know?*

"Hot chocolate?" The shop keeper asked, holding up the chipped teacup as thoughto emphasise his point and distract Noah from the strangeness of his last comment.

"No! I don't want a hot chocolate." Noah strained, trying hard not to burst like a stick of dynamite. The shop keeper's coy smile broke into a beam as he placed the teacup down with a clank.

"Now, now. No need for that." The portly man grinned with a smile in which his teeth were slightly too white and in a way in which there seemed be too many of them. "AsI understand it Lottie will be seeing the High Council tomorrow. Maybe they'll give yousome insight."

Noah's jaw dropped. *How did he know?* Noah wondered. Almost as though he could read Noah's mind, the shop keeper said with an air offactness:

"Tinkerbell told me. Well done against those cramfardles. They were especially nastyones as I have come to know it." The cuckoo clock began to chime, forcing Noah back to reality once again with arude thudder.

"But…but--" Noah's head was beginning to swim with so many questions he didn't know where to start. *Finally, answers.* He thought to himself with the relief you feel when youfind an object after thinking you've lost it for good.

"Take a seat." The shop keeper grinned. "I'll tell you the whole story."

***

Lexivarians, as one might believe, are those who eat words. With a delicate mix of sounds and symbols, the words can come together to make quite a filling meal. Often a lexivarian is accused of being deficient in vitamins, minerals or particular food groups. However, if a lexivarian supplements their lexi with the right auxiliary herbs, they can often live long and happy lives. Lottie stood up from the rocking chair, her head bubbling with excitement as much as the cauldron above the fire was bubbling. She took a place at the long chestnut table and smiled brightly up at Peter.

"I've never eaten words before!" She gurgled, knotting a big spotted napkin round her neck like a bib. "What do they taste like?"

Peter placed a large steaming bowl of lexi down. Lottie peered down into the bowl and couldn't help but be reminded of an alphabet spaghetti on toast she would eat as a child every Thursday evening with her family. This differed slightly in the sense that it was a broth-like and the lexi bobbed at the top like a dumpling might.

"Try them and see." Peter smirked, as he took the space opposite Lottie.

Slowly, Lottie dipped her spoon into the broth and pulled out a large "crunch". She bit into it, and it immediately crunched like a slice of carrot. Her eyes widened and she began to tuck into the broth like there was no tomorrow. The "slurps" tasted were wet and thick but filling in a way that yogurt fills a person. The peppering of auxiliaries herbs "do" and "have" added a texture that she couldn't quite pin down. But her favourite morsels with the flavoursome adjectives. Some were rich and juicy; others were creamy and light. The balance of the lexi danced and sang in her mouth as she gobbled the bowl up, almost without stopping to breathe.

Peter chuckled as he watched Lottie polish off the dish and look sheepishly up and though she wanted more. Peter stood and indulged the whim with the care of any devoted host. As Peter placed down the second bowlful of lexi, a small tinkle distantly sounded, and Peter looked up at the window. Tinkerbell had arrived and seemed to be whizzing around in circles, tinkling like a bicycle bell.

"Tinkerbell!" Peter smiled.

Lottie looked up; her face covered with spattered letters across her face. She gulped down the mouthful and wiped her face with her sleeve.

"Oh really? That's great news!" Peter cheered, jumping up and holding himself up in the air. Lottie watched as the young man did a little celebration wiggle that strongly reminded her of Noah's victory dance when he won a game of Monopoly.

"What?"

"Your enlister is with the summoner." Peter grinned, slowing lowering himself to the floor and trying to contain his excitement.

"Noah's with the summoner? Can I see him?" Lottie's eye lit up like a candle in a dark room.

Tinkerbell began summersaulting into the air again and flipped in many different directions. Peter watched; his eyebrows furrowed as he began to translate the movements.

"Tinkerbell has been given very strict instructions from the summoner that we go to the High Council tomorrow. Hopefully, there's still some time left as flying will take a lot of energy." Peter answered firmly.

Tinkerbell bounced up and down tinkling more slowly. Peter folded his arms and nodded thoughtfully as though he was being told some incredibly confidential information that must not be passed along.

"Yes…yes…I suppose she could?" Peter's voice trailed off as he turned towards Lottie, tilting his head slightly. Lottie pointed at herself and gulped. She'd decided to fill her mouth with a large heapful of lexi and now couldn't speak.

"How confident are you with the Toolio of Imangery?" Peter smiled.

***

Since the independence of Wheyshaven in 1865, the world has since been split into different regions. Wonderland, Neverland and Oz are most well-known outside of Wheyshaven, but the other regions also thrive with their own stories and cultures. Wonderland is placed the North-East-Down-Upon-Thamesliest on the map while Oz is on the complete opposite end. It was rumoured that the Queen of Heart and the Wizard of Oz had been courting and after things ended messily the Wizard need Oz needed to flee as far away from Wonderland as possible as means to keep the Ozions safe from any execution so Oz was remapped accordingly. But this was never formally confirmed by anyone with any power and officials reported it was for economic growth the remapping needed to happen. Neverland, however, is not on the mainland island and most Wheyshavenarians ignore it as a region, largely it's not tied to the mainland but partly because of the way the Neverlanders never quite follow the etiquette of the wider world and dance to a rhythm of their own pipe.

"Neverland? Why is it *there?*" Count Shwangle the One-liest spat as though they had eaten something rotten and needed to clean their mouth out quickly.

"Seems it's been to the Orchard of Ewetrees and Crabapples too." Count Robsagonn the Tensnoot wondered out loud.

"The summonee travelled there fast. No one can travel at that speed without…" Count Shwangle the One-liest's voice trailed off like the end of a song that fades out.

"Without the Toolio of Imagery." Count Robsagonn the Tensnoot finished. (They weren't finishing Count Shwangle the One-liest's sentence to be help, it was a just a pet peeve of theirs if a sentence wasn't finished.)

"Goodtoads." Count Shwangle the One-liest exclaimed, jumping up in the air like they had been struck like lightening. Quickly, they stuck their wing into their satchel and pulled out the potatagram and started twisting the eyes of the potatagram like a radio button.

"What are you doing?" Count Robsagonn the Tensnoot yelled, jumping up from the wheely chair. The force from the jump was so great, the wheely chair was forced to wheel off into a corner of the room and a narrowly miss an open portal.

"Calling the summonees enlister!" Count Shwangle the One-liest explained dodging the rabbit's lunge with surprisingly agility.

"You can't call the summonees enlister, it's against protocol." Count Robsagonn the Tensnoot glared at the green flamingo and uttering 'protocol' as though protocols mattered in this instance.

"I don't care." Count Shwangle the One-liest replied. They stuck the potatagram to their ear and tapped their foot impatiently.

"Right, that's it. I'm going to inform the boss how you're ignoring my orders." Count Robsagonn said in a tone so gloaty one might have thought they'd won a chess game.

But it wasn't checkmate, because Count Shwangle the One-liest wasn't playing CountRobsagonn's game of corporate politics. Instead, the flamingo was pacing quickly around in circles, completely absorbed in their own thoughts.

"Pick up, pick up, pick up!" Count Shwangle the One-liest muttered.

"Are you *listening* to me?" The outraged rabbit yelled, stamping their foot, and foldingtheir arms.

"Yes, yes, yes. A threat of my job." Count Shwangle the One-liest tutted as thoughthey were swatting away an annoying fly from the room with a rolled up newspaper.

"I'm warning you--" Count Robsagonn the Tensnoot seethed through gritted teeth."And I'm warning *you*." Count Shwangle the One-liest hissed with the venom of an acidic flaggawart.

"If the summonee is with Peter Pan, it means the lost boys have sided with the trickster! *Don't you see?*"

The white rabbit sank back, ears flopping to the sides and colour draining from their white fur, so they looked almost grey.

A crackled raspy voice piped up through the potatagram with a menacingly cheerychirpiness.

"Count Shwangle the One-liest, I suppose?" The antique shop keepers voice rangwith the glee. "Let's chat."

Chapter Levens

Bobsweese

When you are faced with a problem such as the problem Count Shwangle the One-liest faced, it is generally advised that you keep your calm and proceed the conversation with an air of certainty, even if you have absolutely no idea what it is you are doing. However, Count Shwangle the One-liest did not proceed with any calmness or any sense of certainty. It is sometimes recorded that Count Shwangle the One-liest that they ran around the Control Room screeching until Count Robsagonn the Tensnoot took the lead on the situation. In other versions, Count Shwangle the One-liest used such unsavoury language that even the sailiest sailors would turn beetroot. While cannot say for sure what was exactly said this is how I imagine things to have unfolded…

"Grobhobbins to you. You can't shropeet me to talk." Shwangle spat with the disgust you have when you're forced to talk to that one person who vexes you to the inner core of your being. You know that one person I'm talking about. No judgement, we all have one.

"Well, well. well." The trickster mused with the smugness of the gloating brottleswatch. "Aren't you brave? Here I am with the enlister and Pan with the summonee and you have the nerve to be icer than a freezing tansworm - _"

"Tweeplets to you. Pan--" Count Shwangle the One-liest retorted.

Before the Trickster had time to reply, the sounds of shattering pot smashed through the crackling radio of the potatagram. The sound of static rushed into the air with the chaos of a spontaneous flashmob. Count Shwangle the One-liest thumped the eye of the potatagram forcefully in the hope to gain signal but nothing happened.

"Any other bright ideas?" Count Robsagonn the Tensnoot glowered as they pulled a large golden watch from their waistcoat. "Now we've lost communication with the enlister and the summonee is in enemy hands. You truly are doing an otterslight job at reasonable--"

"Chattle to you and your status." Count Shwangle the One-liest erupted with such volcanic strength, the white rabbit sank back, ears flopping towards the ground like eggs being dropped from a great height. "I don't see you helping."

As Count Robsagonn the Tensnoot cooking up a strong defence to the thunderous accusations, a glittering shimmer caught their eye.

"Twickers of the light abeen the troutentrue." Count Robsagoon the Tensnoot murmed, the white rabbits whiskers curling into spikes of different directions. "You're here? What in…"

"Silly old rabbit…" A voice giggled from behind Count Shwangle the One-liest.

Count Shwangle the One-liest narrowed their eyes into slits, turning their head as slowly as cold treacle to follow the gaze of the shiverly quiverish rabbit. Before the green flamingo stood a young man with sandy hair which seemed to be nested together in knotted curls. His eyes gleamed sapphire and shone with such glimmer that diamonds were put to shame.

"You didn't deposit the summonee so I just wanted to check…" The young man's voice trailed off as his eyes seemed to acknowledge the unusuality of his surroundings. A faint shrill of the rooster crowed from Count Shwangle the One-liest's satchel, jolting the young man back to focus.

"Peter joined the Trickster. We need to the summonee, and we need the summonee now." The words slipped from the man's lips and cascaded towards the collectors with urgency. Silence and stillness drilled back. The two collectors shifted from foot to foot, avoiding eye contact but staring in every direction.

"The summonee is with Peter." Count Robsagonn the Tensnoot finally whimpered with a snailish snivel.

The young man's face was spattered for a second with a flash of ruthless terror. The terror you might feel when something shifts in the corner of your eyes followed by a slow creek of floorboards. However, in an instant, the terror vanished and slipped into an expression of stoic neutrality that dulled the sapphires and dimmed their shine.

"I guess I'm going to need the enlister." He muttered.

"But Christopher, you can't--" The white rabbit sprang towards the young man who dodged the lunge with a simple quick side-step. In an instant, Christopher grabbed Count Shwangle the One-liest by their neck and pulled them into a portal in which he had chosen to leap.

***

"I don't really know how--" Lottie admitted, holding the unassuming object towards him to inspect. Peter leaned forward, the shadow of the firelight dancing across his face. As his fingertips were about to clasp around the Toolio of Imagery, Lottie's eyes locked onto Tinkerbell. For the first time, Lottie could make out her figure from the shining light. Tinkerbell had one finger pressed to her lips and her other hand pointing to the door.

Lottie's hand dropped slightly, Peter's eyes snapped up to Lottie's face.

"Everything okay?" His silky warm voice hushed.

"Just had a long day." Lottie smiled, pulling the Toolio of Imangery up in a yawning stretch. "Need to get an early night for the High Council tomorrow." She jumped up from her chair and quickly hurried towards the small wooden door.

"Where are you going?" Peter asked, the silkiness in his voice becoming threadbare and woolly.

The warning tinge sliced into Lottie, buckling her knees. As Peter rose from his chair, his faces shifted into shadow and his brooding eyes blackened and sparkled with clatteringly cold gleefulness. His hands grasped towards the Toolio of Imangery. Tinkerbell shot across the room, accelerating headfirst into Peter's smallest finger.

"Ow!" Shrieked Peter, his fingers blistering with large blue warts that seemed to shine with glittery liquid. Tinkerbell curved, diving towards his face. Peter shot up dipping and diving as he screamed in agony.

Lottie tried to push herself up but her feet were rooted to the spot. The tried to pull her foot up but her ankle become more lodged. As she wriggled and writhed, the higher up the leg rootedness became until her knees were as stiff as planks. Lottie's eyes smashed every wall looking for help.

As Tinkerbell and Peter were dipping and diving, objects of various varieties were clattering and clampering to the floor. Tinkerbell flew up his sleeve and Peter smacked all his body, trying his best to smush the fairy like a fly and a flyswat. Tinkerbell plopped out from his collar and stabbed him in the neck. Sizzling blue boils streamed out from his neck causing a screech as deafening as the rolling thunder.

While Peter yelped, Tinkerbell raced towards Lottie twisting herself round as though she were on a roller coaster. The stiffness in Lottie's legs began to subside and she staggered towards the door. With all the strength how could muster, Peter hurtled towards the door, his skin bubbled like a saucepan on the stove. A particularly large wart from his forehead burst dropping oozing oil across his face and dripped his eyes. Hissing wisps of smoke competed well with Peter's cries of agony although the cries of agony ultimately won the battle of loudest sound.

Not losing a second more, Lottie grabbed the door handle and flung it open. She raced into the darkness. She raced. She raced. She raced some more. She raced and raced until she could race no more.

The poison used by Tinkerbell is not often used by fairy-kind. Fairies are better known for showering Wheyshaven with fairy dust and navigating different regions though a variety of luminous plants. However, when a fairy deems a point in crisis, they may choose to inject a dose of "bobsweese". To describe the different effects of this poison is a pointless exercise because each fairy produces a different strand which can have a range of different effects and therefore only the fairy will know the effects of their bobsweese.

***

"Hurry!" Diddly Brush called from the toppiest shelf of the antique shop.

Noah tugged at the labyrinth of tiny Christmas lights that were knotted around his ankles tightly. He grunted as the knots he seemed to untangle seemed to breed and multiply into other knots further down the line he went.

It must be noted, this was not Wheyshavenarian magic but just the logic of Christmas lights we have in our attics, cupboards or anywhere you keep your Christmas lights. In the same way that every Christmas we might tidy our Christmas lights after our festivities, no matter how neatly we have prepared them for the following year, they are always knotted.

The shop keepers body began to stir within the shattered remains of his chicken decorated teapot.

"The trickster will be up if you don't move!" Diddly Brush remarked as though Noah had not yet collected these points together.

Finally, Noah threw off the final lights and darted through the maze of objects towards the door.

"Excuse me." The toothbrush screeched with the rightful indignation of a being who felt a ride in a pocket home was a small price to pay for helping out.

Noah whizzed towards the toothbrush and made a leap to grab it. The toothnbrush plopped neatly into his hand and Noah began to race back through the hodgepodge of thingybits.

"Stop!" Diddly squarked, shaking as hard it could in Noah's tight grip.

"What?" Noah launched back, his mind very much occupied on the fact the shop keepers eyes looked like they had been flickering open and at any moment now, he would soon be standing.

"The book!"

Noah's swerved again away from the shop door and tornadoed his way to the counter. Instead of gracefully navigating his way through the unusual odgebodges, Noah stream rolled his way through every table and low hanging lamp until he was at the counter. He snatched the heavy book with a heave and pulled it to his chest tightly. Very tightly. Tighter than the constriction of a dramslite on its withering dinner.

Cuckoo. Cuckoo. Cuckoo. The cuckoo clock chirped from the wall.

"Not so fast." A rasping voice chuckled.

The shop keepers fez toppled and teetering as the man seemed to drag himself towards Noah and Diddly with alarming speed.

"You don't know what you're doing!" The shop keeper gloated as reached out a hand. His eyes were wider than it looked his sockets could hold, his nostrils flaring with the breath of caves that any cramfardle would have appreciated.

Meow.

The shop keeper froze.

"Go!" Diddly screamed. Not taking a moment to consider what was happening, Noah bolted towards the door for a third time. He struggled through the mess of shattered glass and gooey oils but then tore the door open which such force that the bell dropped to the floor with a mighty clatter. Diddly squawked, squeaked and squealed as Noah seemed to gallop with speeds that he didn't know he could reach through a mess of urban spaghetti.

After what had slipped into an immeasurably long period of time, Noah vaulted through a park gate and suddenly dropped to a slow pace of a gentle plod. Noah dropped his body onto a fading bench that had a plaque that read:

"Dedicated to Mary. A loving mother, grandmother and great-grandmother. She will be missed."

Diddly wriggled with the kind of boogey seen at weddings that forced out of Noah's grip and to land on his lap.

"Now what?" Noah panted, his breath choking to beat away the dull ache of the growing stitch in his side.

"We need the manual it's the…"

"But it's gone. We don't know--"

Meow.

"Goodtoads! Leicester, extranabblenabbulous!"

Chapter Elvewth
The Knave's Riddle

A small creature prowled towards Noah and Diddly, amber eyes shining with flicks or turquoise.

Meow.

The cat stopped, pausing for a moment. Silence.

Meow.

"Follow them." Diddly hissed.

Noah rolled his eyes. From as far back as he could remember, he has always been suspicious of cats and this cat seemed more suspicious than most. While he believed most cats had a secret scheme, this particular cat seemed to have an agenda above all other cats.

Meow.

"Don't be rude." The toothbrush barked with the scorn that seemed to match the flash of the anger in the cats eyes.

Meow.

"Thank you, we couldn't have done it without you." Diddley answered, their voice becoming squashy like an owner does when they talk to their own pet. Before the cat could purr their appreciation and validation to the toothbrush, their fur bristled, suddenly trotting into the across the grass.

"Follow that cat!" Diddly exclaimed so loudly that a dog walker a little further down the gravelled path stopped and turned her head round.

Noah heaved his aching body up, picking the toothbrush up and pulling the big purple leather book to his chest again. The cat seemed to be a dot now but turned its head towards as an invite. Noah jogged towards the cat. The gravel crunched under his worn trainers with each step he took.

Once again, the cat began to trot again until it reached it reached all hedge then slipped under the gate. Noah paused as he surveyed the battered wooden sign with worn painted letters.

"Really? The Secret Garden?" Noah scoffed. "Bit obvious, isn't it?"

Meow.

"Just go in." Urged Diddley with an edge that warned Noah that may not be the hill he should die on.

Noah pulled the latch open and slipped inside. As he turned to close the door, the hedge seemed to shuffle and shift to close any form door that may or may not have existed.

"No no no. Neves lexi with blank, y, blank, blank, n blank, t!" A voice argued as there was a thump of hands slamming on a table.

Meow.

"How can it one-liest across be 'wopplestomp' with the clue 'Truest on the wofelen'?" The voice insisted with a grain of lemonish sourness.

Meow.

"Exactly." The voice concluded triumphantly.

Noah stared at the long table covered teacups of various sizes. Cakes, biscuits, scones and sandwiches were parked and mishmashed any space that was not taken by a teacup of teapot. A yellow hat peeked over the top of a newspaper.

 Meow.

"It feels like nearly centanhexedem trags[1] I've been on this crossword. With only the one-liest answer to get." The voice behind the newspaper argued.

"The mad hatter?"

Instantly, the newspaper dropped onto the table, causing an array of teacups to topple over and smash onto the floor. A short man with beady marble eyes glowered under eyebrows of a caterpillar quality.

"Excuse me?" He seethed, voice wavering with a rumble. Clouds began to thicken with a musty orange tinge. Pink streak pulled over the sky like a canvas.

"The sky. The sky. Knave of Spades. Look at the sky." Diddly yelped.

The man's eye snapped towards the sky and upon noticing the drawing sunset, he began to weep. From a tiny teapot covered in a blue lily pattern,

---

[1] About 160 years

he pulled a huge silver watch. Noah noticed the minute hand was one minute past six.

"She must be desperate if you're excused." A voice observed, making everyone jump.

The Nave of Spades jumped to his feet, saluting a young man that was emerging from another hedge. Behind the new guest was a sight that Noah didn't realise he wanted.

"Green flamingo!" Noah cheered, racing toward the bird with the same excitement one might embrace an old friend.

"Goodtoads!" Count Shwangle the One-liest screamed as their neck was being strangled for a second time.

"I see you know the collector." The young man beamed with the warmth of a toasty hot water bottle on your belly. He held out his hand to Noah. "Christopher Robin, Summoner of Wheyshaven. Call me Chris."

***

Wheyshavenarians young and old know the rumours of the Neverland woods. It is thought that unless you have been taught the tongue of the forest, the trees will bark at you and leaves will whisper your darkest secrets into the wind. Little is known to the reason why the woodland chooses to do this but it is generally agreed that going through the woods is not advised and therefore flight over or tunnels beneath are the best way to navigate this issue.

Lottie stared through the clearing trying to fight the sense for everything. Tree bark was baking ferociously like a pack of wolves snarling. Whispers of secret of her self-doubt seem to whirl and whizz around the gail and the rain smacked the ground and pushed into her face.

"You're not sure you, are you?" A secret taunt cried, hurtling through the air and streaming into the darkness.

Lottie closed her eyes and warm tears dropped from her face. Large fat droplets of saltiness.

"Ow!" She cried, stabbing her eye with the Toolio of Imangery. Lottie glowered at the black pen. There was nothing interesting about this pen, it looked very much like any pen she could buy at any shop. She inspected the end and noticed a small picture of a flame.

"They don't know where you are." Another doubt screamed as it streamed towards Lottie like an out of control Catherine wheel at a badly organised fireworks night. As Lottie covered her eyes, she snapped the end of the Toolio of Imangery and landed heavily with a thump onto an incredibly hard landing.

"Oof…" Lottie huffed as the echoing thud died down in the chamber.

The chilly air was crispier than a clear cold October morning where mist is rising as you ride through country lanes. From the great panes of glass in the ceiling, she watched the stars while they glittered and glittered, gleamed and beamed and down from a tangerine sky, each star-point turning slightly like cogs in a clock. From the duskerly light Lottie noticed the wall was lined with six enormous dominoes. They stretched from floor to the base of the ceiling like columns that held the heavens.

The first face of the dominoes read: six dots at the top, two at the bottom. The next, four at the top, three at the bottom. The following had five at the top and four at the bottom. Opposite the first domino, the first domino had five at the top, two at the bottom. The next, three at the top, two at the bottom. Finally, six at the top and three at the bottom.

Dung.

As the bassy call of a grandfather clocked chimed the hour, each domino in turned on its head like a gymnast does a handstand. It was only through these domino summersaults; has it ever been observed that the dominos are not an architectural foundation feature but merely decorative. Lottie's eyebrows shot up into her fringe while the dots of each domino face turned to their inverse value with the new lower half bubbled to the top much like a sand timer in when being watched with your head upside down and it looks like the sand up travelling up.

When the dominoes had settled into a deafening state of frozen matter, Lottie gingerly stepped forwards. Her shoe slammed down onto the polished marble and echoes with the grace of a rouge hafflelump thromping through a hushed church.

"Hello?" Lottie called out into the ghostly chamber. Nothing moved. Nothing stirred. Even Lottie's own breath seemed to be held in so should a person have dropped a feather; it would have shattered the silence into unparalleled uproar. The silence droned on until a snap cracked the silence with the such force that Lottie felt the air ripple around her. She spun around to see a small object near her feet. Narrowing her eyes, she leant down slowly to retrieve it from the floor. The closer she got the clearer it became that it was a book that was strewed open with pages facing the floor and the covers pushed out to the sides as though someone had placed it down momentarily to grab another cup of tea.

Lottie flicked through the pages to find drawings and jottings, etchings and sketches cramming up every part of the pages. There were pictures of monsters and mushrooms. Long paragraphs on towns and cities with detailed diagrams of various buildings. Lottie's eyes squinted as she tried to unencrypt the notes. After a few moments, Lottie snapped the book shut leaving a whisp of dust to form like a lonely cloud on a clear August day. She turned the book over and inspected the cover: "Wheyshaven Enlister Manual".

***

Count Shwangle the One-liest pushed Noah away and pulled up their wing like a sleeve towards the Summoner.

"We are still running out of time." The nasally collector shrilled as the rooster chirped again from within their satchel.

"Thank you, Count Shwangle the Tensnoot. As they--"

"One-liest." Count Shwangle the One-liest coughed as blushed teal and scraped their claws into the gravelly ground.

One of the Summoner's eyebrows seemed to have been caught on a fish hooked as it spiked up his forehead like a flooping salmon on a fishing line.

"I am at one-liest status, sir. I failed my twolean exam and--"

"I know, but I have decided to grant you Tensnoot status. I..."

Before the Summoner could go on, the green flamingo's knees gave out and the giant emerald bird collapsed into a heap. Noah dropped the big battered purple book and tapped on Count Shwangle the Tensnoot's beak. Nothing happened. He tried again. Nothing happened. He tried again. Finally, the collector's eyes opened and peered up at Noah.

"Uponjellies," Count Shwangle the Tensnoot apologised in a raspy drone as they carefully pulled themselves up and teeters slightly on their two legs. "What happened?"

"You fainted." The Summoner smiled. "Here, eat this."

From a pocket in his long patched up jacket, the Summoner pulled a small light brown rectangle.

"Flapjack." He explained, after Count Shwangle the Tensnoot had sniffed it, snoffed it, pulled it up to their eyes and crumbled some of it into tiny grains.

"Well, all this is very well. But you're all interrupting my teatime crossword." The Knave of Spades piped up, clearly losing interest in the whole affair and with clear focus on where priorities should be.

"Which clue are you stuck on?" The Summoner asked, wondering over to the table and quizzically exploring the paper.

"Why is a raven like a writing desk?" The Knave of Spades glumped, folding his arms sourly.

"Ah, yes. They quozzled me for a while," The Summoner bobbed his head with an empathetic nod. "'Eyesnot' is the answer."

Chapter Tristean
The Summoner's Song

Meow.

"You're right Leicester. You assemble the High Council." The Summoner's face darkened as the snap of reality pushed him back into urgency as he watched the cat trot across the garden. "Knave of Clubs--"

"Call me Jack, sir. Jack Hatta." The man bowed so deeply, his nose dug into the gravel ground while his hat remained stuck to his head as though stuck on with extra sticky stick tape that from the stickiest region of stickfourne.

"Jack," The Summoner nodded absently, "Do you still do your dealings with the Lost Boys?"

Jack stood bolt up right and flung his hands into this knickerbocker pockets. His eyes narrowed as though weighing up the options of a very challenging opportunity.

"Why?" Jack answered curtlier than a curdled curt tart.

"Goodtoads!" Count Shwangle the Tensnoot huffed, folding their arms tightly and tapping their foot with the irritation of a parent who is waiting for their child to finish tidying their room. "Enlister, where is the summonee?"

Noah jumped, surprised on being called to join the conversation. While he wouldn't admit it, he had lost the trail of what was going on and instead was eyeing up a couple of cakes to gobble and a teacup to guzzle while those that were in the know could figure out what the plan was. Now, suddenly in the spotlight, he blinked.

"Er…" He placed Diddly Brush down next to a teapot and leafed through the pages. Pages and pages of scribbles had been inked since he last checked.

"Aha! She's…" His voice trailed off while his eyes scanned, re-scanned and re-re-scanned the page. "In the Domino Towlett with the Wheyshaven Enlister manual."

The Summoner's head dropped to the floor, he eyes seemed to radiate such a calm energy that Jack fell to the floor and crawled quickly under the table.

"What do you mean 'With the Enlister Manual'?" Count Shwangle the Tensnoot squawked, racing towards Noah then pushing him away so they could read the final few sentences for themself.

"Tensnoot, Diddly you to go Oz and meet us at for the High Council." Count Shwangle the Tensnoot grabbed Diddly dropped them onto their shoulder and hopped from foot to foot with such agility you might have thought they were trying to walk on hot coals.

"Goodtoads." Count Shwangle the Tensnoot gasped as they began to spin and turn, picking up gusts of air as they built traction. Air blew harder and faster until they were in the centre of an air tube which pulled the flamingo into the air and the tube rumbled and rambled tossing the collector in a number of different directions. Diddly Brush clung onto the satchel with all their might and yelled word Count Shwangle the Tensnoot couldn't hear.

After a few minutes that stretched and warped in a way that both dragged on and was over in the time of a blink, Count Shwangle the Tensnoot and Diddly found themself dropping out of the air and landing in the middle of a street.

Shops were boarded up with wood that was covered in thick green moss. The eerie quietness was broken by the final gusts of wind pulled lonely newspapers with green font across the road like a tumbleweed.

"This can't be right; we're meant to be in Oz." Diddly squealed, their brushes clearly unimpressed with the grottiness of scene around them.

"Welcome to the City of Emeralds."

***

Until this very point, *The Wheyshaven Enlister Manual* had stayed outside the realm as a means of peace between the different regions since the independence of Wheyshaven. The detailed reasons for this had been decided among the High Council and had not been spread out into the wider news but there were suspicions around the information inside. Some believed it to be a collection of research by a nosy creature, others believed it to be a legendary script that was only passed to enlisters when the time of a summonee was rising in the stars, other rumoured it to hold the deepest secrets of the world and therefore holding the book would give one person ultimate knowledge and by extension power.

As Lottie opened the book again, the Toolio of Imangery glowed an outline of banana yellow, smashing through the duskish light. The closer she placed the pen towards a page, the brighter the glowing outline grew. When the nib touched the diagram explaining how larvae butterfly grow and spread into bread-and-butterflies, a block of butter jumped out of the page and whipped and zipped through the air. The butter flew left and right, up and down. The butter flew sideways and hideways, dideways and chideways. Chipling and champling at different angles. Lottie jumped up together her best to catch the butterfly while her feet echoed loudly through the chamber. When her fingers did reach around to grab it, the butter was too greasy to hold and the butterfly slipped through her hand like a wet soap bar in the bath.

"There it is!" A gruff voice barked with a grind from behind her.

Lottie spun around. In the distraction of the flying butter, she had failed to notice the small army of dalmatians that were seeping from the domino dots. They stood on their hind legs wearing silver collars alongside such scouring scowls, the scour in your kitchen would have felt ashamed. Silence.

"Aren't you going to take it to our mistresses?" The grandfather chimed from the corner.

Lottie felt a flash of annoyance towards the grandfather clock. *Why had it not piped up before?* One of the dalmatians strode up to her, eyes blazing with the fury that only a person being rudely woken from a nice nap can understand. The dalmatian stopped and sniffed her shoulder. It's tail began wagging before it dropped down to all four paws and pranced around like a dog inviting a play. After a few seconds, the whole army were on all fours, either jumping excitedly or rolling onto their back for a fuss.

"Goodtoads." The grandfather clock groaned. Lottie was certain if the grandfather clock had had hands that it could use to facepalm itself with, it would have done so.

Dung.

The colossal chime echoed through the chamber and caused a tremor down the walls.

"Yes, thank you Laurance." An elderly voice yawned from the shadows of a domino.

"Was that really needed at this hour?" Another voice agreed angrily.

Lottie searched for the owners of the voices when she noticed two elderly women clambering down a ladder. One was in a wearing a nightgown with curlers in her greying hair, the other was wrapped in a red dressing down with a green hairnet. The squabbled about their aching joints while they climbed down the ladder and stretched where they could when their frayed slipped were on solid ground.

"Wendy." The elderly lady in the nightgown smiled, she pointed to the lady in the dressing gown. "This is Dorothy."

"Call me Dotty." Both ladies reached out their hands for a handshake but it had seemed Lottie had forgotten all form of manners and just stared between the ladies.

"You shake it, dear." Wendy croaked. This instantly jump started Lottie's memory of basic politeness and she clasped the hand of Wendy and Dotty as well as she could do while she was holding the book and the pen. After a few seconds, the three women beamed at each other.

"Tea?" Dotty offered.

But before Lottie could answer, the moment was perfectly ruined by the rogue butterfly as it whizzed and fizzed with top speeds through the air between the all the dogs.

"Get it!" Dotty chirped and a dalmatian guard hurled itself towards the butterfly and gulped the insect in one large mouthful. Wagging its tail with the pleasure of a particularly happy dog, the dog licked its lips and trotted towards Dotty and Wendy.

"Shall I put the kettle on?" Wendy asked, stretching the type of stretch that always makes you feel better and yawned the kind of yawn that you yawn when you are still awakening up from a deep slumber.

***

After Count Shwangle the Tensnoot's whirlwind has faded into a few playful leaves dancing in small circles, Chris turned towards Noah.

"Come on. We've got work to do." Chris began to stride towards the garden arch in the middle of the pond. He skipped over the stepping stones as though he were doing a hopscotch and landed in the middle with a bow.

"Again, again!" Called a bunch of cosmos from a flowerbed, fluttering their leaves.

"Yes, yes. Again!" Another cried with a daisy patch from the lawn.

Noah jumped as the garden began to clammer and plead with admiration and desperation for Chris to perform again. Instead of resisting, Christopher Robin raised his arms like lion tamer calming the nerves of a lion in a circus ring and the secret garden hushed.

Chris began to sing a rhyme carrying such an expression you would have thought he was confessing some classified information out to the world.

"Fire of hearts and winds of Oz,

The Tweedles born outside the crozz,

Twins of the forest their blood is blue,

A fight did break them in two,

When wizard and queen combine together,

Then twins unite to complete the weather,

An enlister to ashtree a pheonix arises,

Summonee to shield for compromises,

Two books and quill completed adored,

For they are far mightier than the sword."

The garden was silent. Noah still remains unsure about what exactly compelled him to do so, but he began to clap and cheer. After a few seconds he realised no one has cheering or clapping with him so he stopped and scratched his head.

"So, it's true?" Jack whimpered, clambering out from under table, eyes wider than some of the teacup sauces. Chris nodded; head bowed.

"And time is running out…" Chris shook himself and reinstated his signature warm controlled demeanour.

"Are you coming?" He called over to Noah.

"Huh?" He answered, which in this moment, as well spoken as he could manage.

"Are you coming?"

"Where?" There was a pause while Chris gave Noah time to connect the dots. "Oh."

Chapter Quadstean
Wallpapers and Willows

It is often assumed both within our land and in Wheyshaven that when a mighty leader chooses you out to complete a job, you don't consider your other options, but you simply ask what you can do to help. Whether it is a battle of justice or to give your seat up for the bus, the expectation is that you will do what is asked of you, no questions asked. But in this moment, Noah was considering his other options and had more questions than he knew that to do with. He wanted his life back. His normal life. The life where plants didn't talk and flamingos weren't green. The life where cramfardles could be a new hip slang word that he couldn't quite grasp and a life where a toothbrush didn't answer back. He wanted to throw the book to the ground and let it be washed away. He wanted to scream and yell until there wasn't nothing left to give. But he just stood still and silent. Seething with everything and nothing at all both at once.

"What's the matter?" He asked in a soothing voice that would be placed well in a massage parlour.

"I don't get straight answers." Noah glowered at him. "It's all madness and I feel I'm losing my mind."

"Madness is relative to the company you hold and to lose your mind in a world of madness seems the most normalist thing to me." Jack shrugged in a manner that seemed more to himself than the wider company he was holding.

Noah pointed at Jack with an expression of such overwhelming sense of exhaustion and defeat that Jack picked up a teapot and offered it to Noah in a customary form of appeasement. Noah sank onto a chair and held his head in his hands. Jack poured Noah such a large teacup of tea, it took two large teapots to fill the cup. Noah stared at the giant teacup for a moment.

"At what point does a teacup become a teabowl?" He asked finally as he tried to heave the teacup from its saucer. Jack cackled and giggled, he chuckled and chortled until he wept so very uncontrollably that Chris ran over to calm him down.

"Teabowl!" Jack's sniggered, shaking his head with gleeful joy as he slapped his knee.

While the hysterical laughter might have been an overkill for some, Noah found the knave's laughter the medicine he had been missing. He began to titter and pritter until before long he found himself howling and roaring with the infectious playfulness he had not felt in so long he had forgotten how it had felt. Chris beamed as he wanted the two laughing men and had to battle hard against the urge to crack up himself. After a while that cannot be measured, Chris cleared his throat and both the knave and Noah took deep breaths to manage their laughter.

"Are you coming?" Chris asked Noah.

"Who are you seeing first?" Jack interrupted, his face melting into a stern expression that looked like it hadn't been hysterical with laughter. "As you said yourself, all parts of you need to be together and you are very very very much not together."

Noah shook his head violently and stood up.

"I appreciate your offer Christopher Robin but I am not going to let myself be drawn into a load of nonsense. I mean, what was your song even about?"

"Looking for sense and logic! And they called me mad." Jack began to cackle. Chris cast the knave such as icy look that the sapphires in his eyes looked to change shade.

"It was the story of the Tweedle twins."

"Why do I care about the Tweedle twins? Surely they are just bumbling along in Wonderland--" Noah retorted.

"They used to. But after a fight they chose to go their separate ways. However, due to recent events it seems their family secrets are Wheyshaven's lifeline." Chris sighed, shaking his head and folding his arms.

"Can't you just find summon them and decree they get along?" Noah asked.

"It's not quite that simple... We know the whereabouts of both Tweedle twins, but one Tweedle is not crackling the basketwire."

"Which Tweedle twin?"

***

It had been so many moons since Wendy and Dotty hosted a younger guest and even longer since they had been home that they couldn't quite remember anything about the world they left. They had often put the fuzziness of the blurred memories down to old age, but now as they watched Lottie tuck into a warm creamy craquafrome at their dinner table, they somehow couldn't ignore the pang of homesickness that waved over their stomachs. The ache seemed to sail and swish like a huge pirate ship fighting to stay afloat in a particularly gravish storm. Wendy gazed at Dotty with a watery smile and Dotty held reached for Wendy's hand.

"Thank you." Lottie smiled as she wiped the snottle jam from her lips. She would be lying if she said she hadn't been nervous to accept the invite from the two women. But watching the two wives bicker about who should put the kettle on and whose turn it was to feed the dogs, Lottie couldn't help but feel safe in their company.

"Tell us about home." Wendy said, her eyes misty. Dotty rose slightly and pulled a pineapple yellow tissue from a box on the side.

"If you tell me about these." Lottie countered, with a haggle she hoped would not be too rude for her position as a guest in their home. She pointed at the Toolio of Imangery and the *Wheyshaven Manual* which were plompted next to her plate.

While Wendy squinted down at the table, Dotty pulled a pair of teal rimmed glasses from her dressing gown pocket and peered over at the two objects. Her jaw stiffened and she squeezed her lips so tightly together it looked as though she had no mouth at all. Dotty, nudged Wendy forcing Wendy to squint tighter. It became apparent when she had realised what she was looking at because she suddenly wrapped her arms tightly round Dotty and began to whimper. Dotty began to look at the walls.

"What?" Shocked by the sheer fear that had greeted her from her hosts, Lottie's face dropped into the frownliest frown her face could frown.

"Who knows you're here?" Whispered Dotty, her voice trembling.

"Noone. I just--"

"Good. You need to leave Wheyshaven. Now. Go." Dotty's voice grew louder as Wendy's whimpers became quieter.

"But--"

Dotty jumped up and grabbed Lottie's shoulder and pulled her up. Dotty pushed her face close to Lottie's so their noses were almost touching. Wendy pointed at the walls and began to shriek.

"If you don't go now, you will be on trial."

"Trial?"

"The walls have ears! The walls have ears!" Wendy screamed, pointing at the walls. Dotty spun on her heel and charged towards the wooden cabinet in the corner. Seizin her chance, Lottie grabbed the Toolio of Imangery and the *Wheyshaven Enlister Manual*. She clicked the Toolio of Imangery. Nothing happened. She clicked Toolio of Imangery again. Nothing happened.

With foam starting to froth from her mouth, Dotty clawed towards Lottie, roaring. The daisy patterns of the dining room wallpaper had slowly transformed into a pattern of ears. Wendy's face was twisting and setting. As Dotty fell to the floor, she hurled a pair of silver shoes at Lottie. Lottie grabbed them and tore off her own shoes. Dotty writhed and screamed while Wendy arms locked grew.

Lottie pulled on the shoes and grabbed the Toolio of Imangery and *Wheyshaven Enlister Manual* to her chest.

"Love…" Dotty howled in pain that turned to the howl of a dog.

"You…" Wendy roared back, her voice choking.

Instinctively, she clicked the heels together and she smashed up into the air.

The speed in which she moved may have been faster than a cramfardle eating a brain, but it was still long enough for her to hear the wails of the two wives. She closed her eyes and smushed them as tightly together as she could.

From the records, it is hard to tell if the Oxenwell weeping willow and the dalmatian are the regional signs with roots to Wendy and Dotty Dale or if the wives were transformed into these signs as a warning out to other Wheyshavenarians in the region. However, it has become a long practiced superstition that when the sky is tangerine and the stars are turning like cogs in a clock, you must throw a warm creamy craquafrome to a pot and be weary of the wallpaper pattern changing.

***

The rooster called from Count Shwangle the Tensnoot's satchel again which a squawk only reserved for the most urgentest of breaking news. They sighed and tried to grab the rooster from the bag. After a few seconds to grappling with nothing, they finally seized the neck of the rooster and yanked it out. Scarlet and green feathers erupted across the pavement and the rooster glowered up at the green flamingo with a tired glare.

"Rooster, rooster of the mooster, upon what is going on?" Count Shwangle the Tensnoot recieted as quickly as they could.

The news jingle blared so loudly a green tinged rasting from across the street scuttled down into a sewers that seemed to be glowing an unsettling limeluminous shade of emerald. Count Shwangle the Tensnoot yanked on the roosters wattle until it was overperforming at a more reasonable volume.

"The weather-"

"Next."

"Sports-"

"Next-"

"Breaking news: For those of you who have been following the Lottie story, it has been seen fleeing from the Dale wives household. There have been claims that she is wearing Dorothy's silver shoes and does not know what she is doing. Count Robsagonn the Tensnoot was a witness to the incident. Can you tell us more?"

A familiar slimey voice sneered out of the roosters beak:

"Thank you. By the time we had located Lottie, it had taken flight using Dorothy's shoes. The investeragation squad have found a riddle on one of the walls but nothing else yet."

The rooster's voice switched back to the overly pushy voice all Wheyshavenarians were used to:

"Riddle?"

Count Robsagonn the Tensnoot's voice stammered out of the roosters beak, apparently taken off guard by the question and annoyed at themselves for delivering this detail out into the public world:

"Er, yes. Just a riddle. Nothing more. I-I wouldn't think anything of it."

The rooster's voice swapped back to the normal preseenters voice with annoyingly fast speed, making Count Shwangle the Tensnoot's head was beginning to spin as they fought hard to hold on to the train of conversation.

"Come on, we all like a brain tweester here. What it?"

The white rabbit's voice sighed heavily through the roosters beak and then it cleared it's throat:

"Crimes of doors and pictures alike break bread with commonality."

The rooster returned back to the salesy voice:

"Wow, that'll stump the best of us. In other news: The summoner is--"

"Close."

The rooster's break immediately shut but the eyes sharply warned the green flamingo that if they tried to stuff them back into the satchel things could get very unpleasant very quickly. Count Shwangle the Tensnoot placed in the crook of their wing and scanned the bleak streets with the equal enthusiasm most feel when they encounter a bosseltri in the elevationator.

"Where is everyone?" Diddly squeaked from Count Shwangle the Tensnoot's shoulder.

As the green flamingo had completely forgotten about the fact they were with the toothbrush, Count Shwangle the Tensnoot leaped into the air, dropping the rooster onto the floor. Luckily for the toothbrush, they had anticipated this reaction and clung onto the satchel buckles to reduce landing on the floor themselves.

"Why did you just scare me like that?" The green flamingo humffled.

"I didn't mean to, I was just…Why is your chicken crossing the road?"

Sure enough, Count Shwangle the Tensnoot's rooster was sauntering across the yellow brick road with the cockiness of a chicken unaware of its own bravery and heading towards the unsettling limeluminous sewer. Count Shwangle the One-liest zoomed towards the rooster with such speeds that there was almost a flamingo shaped cloud where they were just stood. They grabbed the rooster from the ground and leaped back onto the pavement.

"Goodtoads, why would you do that?" The green flamingo asked flushing deeper green.

Chapter Fivstean

Wonderfless

A little known fact about news roosters within Wheyshaven is that they have are similar to magpies when they see something shiny. They must acquire said shiny object no matter what the cost. This might be a snottle that has just been harvested before they turn they get their signature pink with blue stars pattern. The object could be an oversized dice with mirrored faces that reflect such dazzling light it's nearly impossible to look directly at the dice without a welding helmet. In this instance the shiny object of this news rooster's desire was in fact the unsettling limeluminous sludge that was radiating from the sewer and nothing was going to get in its way.

The rooster lunged it's head towards Count Shwangle the Tensnoot's eyes and with a quick jab, the rooster was free. Whilst Count Shwangle the Tensnoot cursed and tried to blink away the pain, the roosted, pulled a large pile of unsettling limeluminous sludge from the sewer gutter and began to construct a very gooey, very slimy, very sludgy nest. Diddly, who had no anticipated the roosters move, dropped to the floor and squirmed around on the cracked green pavement like a wriggling wriggleswright on their wriggsday.

"How much time have we got?" A shaky voice asked from the ally next to the sewer.

Count Shwangle the Tensnoot stopped dead their tracks and stared towards the ally. They pulled their wing up as though it were a sleeve and checked their watches. None of them were moving. They tapped each one but each watch gazed back with a glazed glass expression on the face. Not a tic. Not a toc.

"How much time have we got?" The shaky voice asked again, a panic started to rise in what sounded like a very meek being.

"Show yourself!" Count Shwangle the Tensnoot answered the talking ally. They seized Diddly Brush from the ground and brandished them like a sword. "I have a toothbrush and I'm not afraid to use it."

"Oh great!" Hissed the Diddly, apparently unappreciative of the fact they had been picked up.

A figure appeared from the darkness of the alley. Upon laying eyes on the new comer, Count Shwangle the Tensnoot gasped the gaspiest gasp and dropped Diddley onto the pavement (an act the toother was even less appreciative of) and folded into a deep bow.

If you hadn't known who this man was, on first impressions you could have been forgiven for thinking this man was far from important. His salty-silver hair had a greasy thickness to it which seemed to be amplified by the disordered disarray the wildness it had collected. The man's bloodshot eyes were redder than a ripe red chilli and looked like they had been burned in such a manner. Tattered and threadbare was somewhat of an understatement to the state of his jade shaded suit and it seemed to hang off the man's frame like a retiring employee counting down their days from a job they had hated for 35 years.

"How much time have we got?" The man asked again, his voice clearly not trying to hide any form of panic.

Count Shwangle the Tensnoot bolted up from their bow and tore their wing back like a sleeve again.

"There isn't any, you're wonderfulness." Count Shwangle the Tensnoot shrieked, matching the panic in the man's voice.

"I think wonderfless is better suited." He sighed, digging his hands into his pocket and drawing out a huge handkerchief with spotted hearts on it. "I didn't mean for this to happen."

***

The wails and screams were still tearing into Lottie's mind as she stared at the huge crowd in front of her. In the distance there seemed to be the sound of a siren but it didn't sound quite like a siren she had heard before. It seemed to be dulled by a water-like distance. Shapes and figures seemed to swirl and writhe beneath her. Flashes seem to thunder towards her as she began to hurtle towards the ground. Everything was both extremely close in a way to press into your personal space in a way no one likes and very very far away. Her body seemed to be moving, being pushed, but she wasn't doing it herself. Autopilot. Screams and shouts. As her eyes scanned over the tidal wave of beings. Their faces were snearing and snarling, jeering and leering, hissing and squissing up at her. They all seemed to melt, meld and merge into one face that was not by any means happy.

What is happening? I don't want this. She thought as the screams of the wives to rampaged her mind with the anger and resentment of a poltergeist who has not yet been appeased.

Before Lottie had time to untangle and unpuzzle the events that seemed to be unfolding at a speed of unimaginable knots, a colossal squawk overpowered the tsunami of faces below and Lottie felt her body being lifted higher into the air with talons grabbing her around the waist.

Making enemies? A familiar warm thought warned with the sternness of a disappointed parent.

"I don't know what's happened--" Lottie protested. The bubbling crowd below seemed was being drowned by the whistling speed of the crashing air around them. "I just--"

I know. The voice soothed, apparently aware they may have been a little too short and a little too harsh for the circumstances.

"What's going to happen?" Lottie whispered as the dainty droppling of her tears evolved into a sob of true ugliness.

You do what you want to do. The griffin suggested with the underhelpfulness Lottie had hoped the animal wouldn't offer.

"But I need--"

Need? The griffin jabbed back, as they swerved up higher to a dizzingly highness. *You need to eat and sleep. You can choose just about anything else.*

Easy for you to say. Lottie thought, sourly as the sobbed began to promote itself to an unsightly wail.

Is it wise to insult an ally? The warm thought asked, pushing the point with such precision and so much compassion that Lottie's sulkiness dissolved into a puddle of guilt.

"I'm sorry." She murmured as she wiped her eyes.

Thank you. Now, what is it you wish to do? The thought asked with a cool businessish tone.

"What can I do?"

You can go home, or you can stay here.

"What happens if I go home?" Lottie asked, glad to finally be able to talk through a potential plan.

The Tweedle Tale becomes truth. The thought answered so casually that Lottie felt the thought would have shrugged should it have been able to shrug.

"Excuse me?"

If you stay, you will be hunted for trial and seen before a judge and jury that will result in either an exaction or banishment. The thought ploughed on as though Lottie had not asked for more clarification and continued to steam with the same laid-back fashion that Lottie felt more unsettled than informed.

"What do you mean?" Lottie protested, a bubbling surge boiling up in such a manner than if she had been a pot of water on the hob, she would have been the ideal boiliness type to poach an egg.

But before Lottie could further jab or poke for any further details, she noticed a little light spec grow on the horizon.

What's that? The wondered to herself, dropping any emotion other than curiosity. As the griffin headed towards the horizon, the spec began to grow. The growing spec seemed to grow until the growing spec went from spec to splodge and splodge to smudge and from smudge to... Lottie gasped.

Purple flames were engulfing a tree like its blossom. The flames seems to dance different shades as each blossom flicked in the breeze. Long licks of fire seemed to hop between deep violet then skip into baby lilac and jump into a relaxing state of plum.

The ashtree has not burned this brightly for some time, phoenix rebirth must be upon us.

***

"What do you mean 'Peter Pan'?" Noah whispered, shaking his head so vigorously you might have thought he were doing an impression of a little ornament with bobblehead.

"I told you he's the--"

"Really. Him?" Noah jumped up from the table like a jack in the box and paced across the lawn, folding and unfolding his arms.

"You can pace all you want but it won't make it untrue." Jack interrupted, pulling a large red straw from under his hat and using it as a toothpick.

"So... where's the other Tweedle twin?" Noah asked with his head down, pacing so quickly the grass began to moan in pain. There was such a long pause tat garden began to titter at Noah's apparent unawareness.

"Has he not caught on?" The jasmine whispered to the ivy.

"We're in even more danger if it can't connect--" A tulip said with a large stingley of a nosey neighbour who is watching events pan out through their net curtons.

"Silence." Chis growled in a manner that was gruffier than the sandpapers of Weasdoon beach. (As a side note, Weasdoon beach is absolutely not a tourist destination anyone should ever consider.)

Upon the silence a slow start of a train of thought set off in Noah's mind and thought train carriages were starting to connect together. It was all build speed fast. Very fast. The thought train was whistling and chugging, turning and swerving through the tunnels and fields of his brain. The train was unstoppable and seemed to ignore any rhyme or reason to any stops or junctions it could be taking.

Noah leapt and grabbed the purple book, tearing it open. The words seemed to mishing and mashing, smashing and smishing in a whirlwind of letters and words. With each cycle of cycling, they seemed to lift off the page and falling out into the garden.

"What's it doing?" A deeply wrinkled groaned with a wheezelyish groan. The leaves had dropped off and it looked very out of place in the otherwise brimming garden.

"Elders." Tutted a young pansy from the flowerbed below.

Thunder rumbled and lightening spewed from the book. Words weren't words anymore but the book now seemed to spitting out objects. Dominoes. Cards. Sand was beginning to seep from the spine and animals of various variety were pouring out. Clocks of all ticking varieties. Yellow gems and heart spotted handkerchiefs.

"Come on…" Noah reached into the book and began pulling more objects out. A mermaid began to flip and flop on the gravel, spewing such language that is has not been recorded.

"Where are you?" Noah gritted his teeth and dug his arm even further up so the book was up to his shoulder now.

The tornado of words and letters, sounds and screams was almost bursting. It seemed to be pressing and pushing. With the might he had never conjured before he pushed his arm even deeper. There it was. With a heave of a pirate pulling an anchor from the seabed. Noah pulled it up. Grunts and moans, gritted teeth and scrunched up face, Noah pulled. Until a brilliant purple explosion streamed from the book flying and into the air.

Noah flew back and landed on the ground with a thrump. The purple fire flew like a firework and cracked like a Christmas cracker. Within a few seconds, the blazed fizzed and popped into an enormous mushroom cloud of black ash.

Cough. Cough. Cough.

Noah watched as two small boys emerge from the ash. One with dark hair, holding a set of pipes and the other fair hair with holding bear. Noah peered around and it seemed to be just him and the two boys in the garden. Jack seemed to have vanished. So had the tea table and the various objects of different varieties.

"Bet you can't catch me, Chris!" The boy with the pipes said, dropping his pipes and immediately speeding up. The fair haired boy instantly dropped the bear and began to chase his brother. The two of them giggled and laughed as they dodged and dived each other.

Noah scanned across the garden, but noticed wasn't moving. The flowers weren't smiling or chattering. They were still but seemed to watch over the two boys with the utmost reverence. He looked up to see the inky darkness of the evening pull further in. A chilly wind bristled.

"Time was always going to end." A voice from the elder tree. "Mad."

"Madness is relative to the company you keep." Noah half-chuckled as he looked up to see the black and white cat sitting up and licking a paw.

Ding ding. Noah's phone buzzed in his pocket. He checked his first pocket, just a collection of fluff and a tissue that was essentially fluff. He checked the other and to his disappointment it was not a potatagram that greeted his eyes but his flat rectangular phone with a cracked screen. Tapping the screen a sight of truest sightliness beholded him. Leaping into the air and thrashing his arms up, Noah proceeded to complete very strange victory dance. Double checking the screen again, he found his eyes had not been tricking him but the screen had in fact said what he had though it had said.

Lottie:

Dinner's on the table, where are you?